Country
Wisdom

Country Wisdom

Rosamond Richardson

Kyle Cathie Limited

This book is dedicated to countless unknown philosopher-magicians, mostly women of intuition, who have practised country wisdom down the generations across the world.

Acknowledgements

My thanks to the late Harry Westbury who suggested the idea for this book to Kyle Cathie in the first place. I deeply regret that he never saw it published. I am indebted to Rafi Fernandez, Chantek McNeilage, Barbara Lumsden, Annie Holland and Marlise Riding. Special thanks also to E. Barry Kavasch, Yvane, Françoise, Joan, Emanuele, Lionel and Hilda, Jenny, Diana, Angela, Oona, Inge, Robyn, June, Mineke and Olga. I am grateful to numerous friends and acquaintances who tolerated my endless questions and demands whilst I was researching this book, and who went to some lengths to find material for me. Thanks too to the team at Kyle Cathie Limited who have put so much energy and skill into producing this beautiful book.

First published in Great Britain in 1997 by
Kyle Cathie Limited
20 Vauxhall Bridge Road
London SW1V 2SA

ISBN 1 85626 232 4

Text © 1997 Rosamond Richardson
Photography © 1997 Michelle Garrett
Designed by Robert Updegraff
Home economy by Jaques Clarke and Susie Theodorou

Rosamond Richardson is hereby identified as the author of this work in accordance with Section 77 of the Copyright, Designs and Patents Act 1988

A CIP catalogue record for this title is available from the British Library

Printed and bound in Italy by Editoriale Johnson S.p.A.

If you would like to contribute a piece of traditional wisdom that has been passed down through your family in a sequel to this book, please send it to Rosamond Richardson at

PO Box 56, Saffron Walden, Essex, UK, CB11 4HT
or e-mail Rosamond @ webserve.co.uk

Important Notice

This book contains information on a wide range of herbs and remedies that can be used medicinally. It is not intended as a medical reference book, but as a source of information. Before trying any remedies, herbal or otherwise, the reader is recommended to sample a small quantity first to establish whether there is any adverse or allergic reaction. Remember that some remedies which are beneficial in small doses can be harmful if taken to excess or for a long period. The reader is also advised not to attempt self-treatment for serious or long-term problems without consulting a qualified doctor or health practitioner. Neither the author nor the publisher can be held responsible for any adverse reactions to the recipes, recommendations and instructions contained herein, and the use of any remedy or herbal derivative is entirely at the reader's own risk.

Contents

Introduction

Country Wisdom is a lively and varied compilation of recipes and domestic lore, as passed down through the generations. This practical, commonsense wisdom, collected from all over the world, offers many keys to everyday life, because country 'wisdom' is halfway between common sense and science and touches on both. Our grandparents, the wise women and men of the past, were practical philosophers who understood how things work, rather than why. Their innate wisdom was grounded in observation and experience. Subsequent generations have made use of this inherited wisdom because it works, and not necessarily – although there are many exceptions – because it has been 'proved' by the criteria of science. A certain element of mystery may thus enter into this wisdom, it may not be proven but it should not necessarily be dismissed either, even by experts in the field. It is in a category of its own and that, along with an occasional flirtation with superstition, is part of its eternal charm.

The response from people whose grandparents or parents have used practical lore in house or garden, sometimes adding the language of symbols, stories and proverbs, shows vividly how it has become woven into the fabric of everyday family life. I gleaned some of this wisdom in response to a world-wide request on the Internet for personal stories. Other gems were collected from friends and acquaintances of many nationalities, so this book is an accumulation of oral sources, family 'commonplace books', small unpublished herbals and local publications. What became clear is that traditional country wisdom is still very much alive in rural areas, but fast disappearing with the encroachment of city life and the genesis of a new 'urban folklore'.

This wisdom appears in slightly different but recognizable guises around the globe, and has a universal place in society. One of the great mysteries is that similar ideas and customs occur in distant places among people who have no cultural contact with each other, and spring from entirely different races and civilizations – even in the most remote places on earth. 'Truth is one, the sages speak of it by many names', in the wisdom of the Vedas. Identical concepts, astonishingly constant and whose roots go back into antiquity, appear to come from a universal, collective source. The 'basic magic ring of myth' has no respect for boundaries. Thus, the wisdom of a Mexican healer mirrors a cure 'discovered' by a farm worker in East Anglia: the former used cobwebs to seal the cut umbilical cord after childbirth; the latter pulled curtains of cobwebs from the barn walls when a colleague was

badly cut by farm machinery – they staunched the wound and his prompt action saved a life. These stories, two of many, touch on a vast subject, incalculable in size, infinite and universal, which can never fit between the covers of one book. We can offer but a taste, yet even this is a rich feast.

This book is a celebration of a mostly female culture, of a heritage based on nature and practised by country women who were closer to the usefulness of plants and the cycle of natural rhythms than we are today. They lived their lives without constant reliance on technology and chemicals, but according to nature and the seasons, using a combination of common sense, intuition and inherited wisdom. Some might call them witches, but: 'It behoveth a magician, and one that aspires to the dignity of that profession, to be an exact and very perfect philosopher', according to Giambattista della Porta, an Italian herbalist writing in the seventeenth century. The multi-faceted arts these women practised offer welcome relief from today's prevailing reductionist approach: now their wisdom fulfils a need, deeply felt by many, to use fewer chemicals, to recycle material, to 'waste-not-want-not', and to be less dependent on processed goods.

Rich with symbols and yet rooted in practicality, this country wisdom, with its awareness of nature and its relationship to folklore, contains the possibility of fulfilling another universal need, that of giving significance to the mysterious, thus empowering us to influence our own lives. So grounded in pragmatic experience is this art that much of the wisdom of our grandparents is still applicable to us today: it works. This collection is no arcane whimsy, but essentially a 'how to' book,

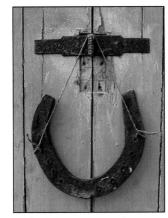

translated where necessary into today's terms, although some superstitious touches are included for fun: old wives' tales, love lore, and legends about cats are not overlooked.

The book looks at gardening lore and weather, how herbs can be used as gentle medicines, the use of plants for simple cosmetics, in making traditional wine cups and brews, how certain plants always had their part to play in the household whether it be for cleaning and fragrances, or for celebrations. And there is a section on how to use many wild plants for the larder and freezer, making the most of an annual country harvest which is autumn's gift to us all.

This is a book to use, to amuse, to be enchanted by, to enjoy. Its richness lies in its variation as much as its abundance: fully illustrated with beautiful photography it offers the key to a magical yet practical world which is ours for the exploring.

HOME AND HEARTH

Mid pleasures and palaces though we may roam,
Be it ever so humble, there's no place like home.
John Howard Payne (1791-1852), from his play *Clari*

Whether your home is ever so humble, or a palace, or something in between, it is your castle. If you live in a city or town you may dream of making your home in the countryside with its inky starlit nights and fresh air, to feel the changing climate through the turning seasons, to be subject to the moods of nature to which urban life is less exposed. Whether your home is a refuge from pollution and noise, or looks out on to the lanes and fields, looking after it takes a significant amount of time and energy. We learn some lessons from the experience of our mothers and grandmothers, the rest we pick up as we go along. There is a rich store of wisdom from the days before heavy chemicals were used in cleaning and washing, and some of it is just as appropriate to today's world as it was then and can be updated to modern needs. I have collected tips from people who live or have lived in far-flung corners of the world – Singapore, Zimbabwe, Brazil, St Helena, China, Holland and Germany as well as the UK and USA. What is surprising is how many of the practical tips overlap, even though they originate from unconnected cultures. For example, salt recurs universally, and lemons are ubiquitous.

North American Indians had a tradition that salt could be used to overcome bad energies in the house: sprinkling salt in the corners of each room creates a protective circle which invites in the Spirit of the Wind. Interestingly, Jews have a custom of presenting salt (and bread) to the new owner of a house on their first visit. And there is an English tradition of sprinkling salt in front of the threshold before you take ownership.

There are endless touches that constitute the art of home making. The use of colour, or the way you arrange the furniture and ornaments, expresses something about who you are. Rudolf Steiner said that 'you never see a straight line in nature, so try imitating the curves of the natural world in your furniture and fittings'. Bringing houseplants into the home increases the healthy ions in the atmosphere; candlelight can transform an occasion; and an open fire gives cosiness and focus to cold winter nights. The family festivals that punctuate the year have as their focus hearth and home, underlining the central importance of the home-making aspect of our family life.

The task of keeping the home fresh and clean is eternal. Using natural as opposed to chemical ingredients makes your house smell good, and it will not be polluted by some of the toxic gases given off by synthetic cleaners. Cheap and easy to use, these materials really do work, the natural way, and are just as handy for today's computer keys as they were for scouring the pans before the days of stainless steel. You can control household pests, keep the bathroom spotless, banish unwanted cooking smells and remove stains without resorting to an array of chemicals. Try it: it works.

KITCHEN

'A general anarchy prevails in my kitchen', wrote the lugubrious Dr Johnson: perhaps he needed a touch of Feng Shui, which prescribes the kitchen to be airy, spacious and well-lit. Associated with the health of the family, it should be a calm environment with as many natural materials as possible – cane, raffia, wood and clay. Green houseplants deflect bad energy and ionize the atmosphere, although spiky cacti are not auspicious (anything with sharp angles on it deflects good energy). Keeping the kitchen clean the natural way without resorting to heavy chemicals will keep it smelling good. Friends in the USA, Kenya, Germany and Holland, to name but a few places, have contributed their tips on how to keep this important centre of the home clean, bright and fragrant using ordinary kitchen ingredients.

Dealing with Strong Smells

To remove strong smells on wooden boards after chopping onions, garlic or fish, rub the area with the cut side of half a lemon. If your hands smell strongly of garlic, rub some English mustard powder into them before washing them, and this neutralizes the smell. To clean pans in which you have cooked fish, and which still retain the smell, rub well with a cut lemon after washing, then rinse thoroughly.

If the bread bin smells musty, wipe it with a little white vinegar on a damp cloth and leave it open to dry. This will also get rid of any mildew. For smells in the fridge, leave a bowl filled with cat litter, bicarbonate of soda, or charcoal: they all absorb smells. If the microwave gets smelly, half-fill a small bowl with water, add 3–4 tablespoons of lemon juice, and run on high for 1 minute. Remove the bowl and wipe the oven clean.

If the smell of cigarette smoke lingers, light a candle for half an hour or so to get rid of the smell. To lessen the smell in the first place, put a dish of water mixed with vinegar in a discreet place near to the smoker, and some of the smell will be neutralized.

Simmering spices gives the kitchen a beautiful aroma and disguises unwanted cooking smells. Simmer cinnamon or cloves with a little brown sugar in water over a very low heat.

Damp Cupboards

Fill a coffee can with charcoal briquets, punch holes in the sides and lid, and place it in the cupboard to absorb moisture. Or you can tie pieces of chalk together and hang them inside the cupboard. If you have a damp outside wall, plant sunflowers against the wall. A Dutch friend who lived on marshlands told me this, and I tried it in a cottage where I used to live. It worked, and the sunflowers gave me a lot of pleasure as I worked in the kitchen.

Cast-iron Pans

Cast-iron pans rust easily, and the best technique to prevent this happening is to rub them with vegetable oil after washing, and dry thoroughly with kitchen paper. If however they do rust, rub the area with a solution of 1 tablespoon citric acid in 600 ml (1 pint) water, and this will remove it. A Norwegian friend told me that her grandmother boiled pots and pans with horse-droppings to prevent rust!

Aluminium and Stainless Steel Saucepans

A woman in the village who has been doing cleaning work all her life told me that for discoloured pans she simply boils up rhubarb or lemon juice to remove staining. If the bottom gets burnt, fill with cold water and leave to stand for an hour. Then add some borax powder or cream of tartar and boil up. The burnt food will come away quite easily without injuring the pan.

Alternatively fill the pan with water and add a sliced onion plus a tablespoon of salt. Boil for 10 minutes, then leave to soak overnight. The residue will wash away easily.

For marks on stainless steel, rub with a handful of flour, then polish with a soft cloth. If it is badly marked, use a scouring pad and lemon juice.

Copper

When heavily tarnished, an English country remedy is to rub the coat of grime with crushed rhubarb leaves, or use the cut side of a lemon dipped in fine salt. A Belgian friend suggests you fill a plant-spray bottle with vinegar, spray it on and allow it to stand for several hours, then rub clean.

If copper turn green, remove the verdigris with a solution of ammonia, using rubber gloves.

Cleaning the Oven

Everyone's least favourite task is made easier if you rub it clean with a damp cloth dipped in bicarbonate of soda. For heavy soiling, mix 1 tablespoon of paraffin with 2 tablespoons of salt and scrub into the staining. Rinse off with hot water and washing soda (using rubber gloves).

Pouring salt on to food-spills on the stove while you are cooking prevents them burning. This also works inside the oven and is very useful – I am constantly having overflows in the oven which burn horribly. This simple treatment prevents the worst of the smells.

Washing Up

For those eternal tea stains on mugs, dip a damp cloth into bicarbonate of soda and rub the stain off. This also works for cigarette stains on china. Use the same treatment for a teapot, or if heavily stained put in a handful of washing soda, and fill up with boiling water. Leave to stand until cool, and this will remove the tannin.

When washing up greasy dishes a useful tip is to add a little vinegar to the water (2 tablespoons per bowl) – it leaves dishes sparkling clean. You can also use lemon juice as a rinse-aid in the rinsing water.

If you have a porcelain sink which needs cleaning, put layers of kitchen paper over the bottom, and saturate with diluted bleach. Leave for 5–10 minutes, then remove the paper and rub clean. The even contact of the bleach, plus the length of time it is left in the soaked paper, cleans up all discoloration and brings up the whiteness of the porcelain. For a stainless steel sink, use a damp cloth dipped in white vinegar to remove water spots. Shine by rubbing with soda water.

To keep the sink in good condition, put a cupful of washing soda down the plughole once a week, and wash it down with a kettleful of boiling water to remove any blockages and keep it clean. For limescale around the plughole, rub the deposit hard with the cut side of half a lemon: the acidity dissolves it away. If you get limescale in the kettle, an old-fashioned remedy is to put a marble in the kettle to prevent furring. My method is to cover the element with equal parts of vinegar and water, bring to the boil and leave to stand overnight. Then I rinse it out thoroughly, boil a kettleful and throw away the water before making the first cup of tea.

My mother always used to clean her copper pans with a vinegar-soaked cloth.

Feng shui recommends that bedroom furniture be kept uncluttered, especially around the door, to facilitate the flow of energy into the room.

BEDROOMS AND BATHROOMS

Weary with toil, I haste me to my bed,
The dear repose for limbs with travel tired.
William Shakespeare (1564–1616), *Sonnet xxvii*

You could say that the bedroom is the most important room in the house: we probably spend more time there than in any other single room. Feng Shui calculates the direction that the bed should face according to the year of your birth, whereas Muslims never lie in a bed with the feet pointing towards Mecca, always the head. An English grandmother told me that she had always been told to place the head of the bed to the north and the foot to the south.

In Feng Shui the shape and element of the headboard can make a significant difference to your energy: rounded metal is good for people engaged in paperwork, rectangular wood for professionals, and oval or wavy shapes for artists and musicians. Don't have too many mirrors in the bedroom – if any – because they attract so much energy into the room that you may have trouble sleeping.

In illness the bedroom becomes a particular focus. Put plants or cut flowers next to the sickbed in order to produce more oxygen during the day, and remove them at night when they put out carbon dioxide. Put a bowl of water on the radiator to relieve a dry cough at night, adding some eucalyptus oil if you like. There are some excellent invalid beverages (see pages 178–9), and for a really good night's sleep, drink one of the nightcaps on page 181.

Stains on the Mattress

Moisten 1 tablespoon of powdered starch with a little washing-up liquid and apply to the stain. Leave to dry, then brush off with a stiff brush. Or, wearing rubber gloves, sprinkle a damp cloth with a few drops of ammonia.

Cupboards and Chests of Drawers

My American grandmother left me a chest of drawers made from cedar wood, which is a natural moth deterrent, and I still use it. Line the drawers with fresh paper, and add dried citrus peel or scented bags (see page 104) to keep them smelling fresh and fragrant. This is also a moth-deterrent. Put unwrapped soap into drawers to scent them or make some simple sachets. For a lavender sachet take a handful of lavender buds and place in the middle of a square of muslin. You can add some dried wormwood too, an excellent moth repellent. Gather up the edges, and tie tightly with a satin ribbon.

A Dutch friend described how her grandmother aired musty cupboards and drawers. After removing the contents she hung them up outside on a pleasant day to air. Then she crumpled up newspaper and filled the drawers and cupboards, and left them slightly open for a few days while the paper and ink absorbed damp and smells. Finally she would wipe them out and if possible leave them outside on a breezy day to air thoroughly.

Storing Clothes

The Sultan's clothes from around 1450, kept in the Topkapi Museum in Istanbul, are completely intact and look like new. They are folded in linen and laid flat, kept in the dark, and brought to air once a year. The embroidered silks, brocades, damask with gold and silver thread, and tapestry remain as pristine as five hundred years ago. We can use this simple technique for storing our own clothes.

A Malaysian friend always puts whole cloves – a moth deterrent – into her coat pockets before storing them away for the summer, and into plastic bags with her woollen jumpers. It keeps them far more fragrant than the horrible smell of mothballs.

Mirrors and the Dressing Table

To clean mirrors, apply a few drops of methylated spirits on a damp cloth, then buff with a clean soft cloth. Don't use water as it may run down into the frame and damage the silvering.

A teaspoon of borax plus a tablespoon of washing soda in warm water will keep hairbrushes clean and fresh.

Soak jewellery in a solution of washing-up liquid for a few minutes before cleaning with toothpaste and a fine toothbrush –

this according to an American friend's grandmother in Ohio. Rinse again, and dry off with a hairdryer. Buff with a soft cloth to bring up the brilliance. Diamonds love gin: they sparkle after a good soaking and then brushing with a toothbrush in warm water.

To keep pearls clean, wear them next to your skin as often as possible – the natural oils in the skin polish them.

Bathrooms

Rub liquid detergent on mirrors to prevent them steaming up. When a natural sponge goes slimy, soak it in 1 tablespoon of vinegar to 600ml (1 pint) water. Clean off hard-water marks on tiles or shower doors with neat white vinegar on a soft cloth. Leave for 20–30 minutes, then rinse off.

Rub stubborn marks in the bath with turpentine or white spirit and rinse with hot washing-up solution. For old stains on baths, use equal quantities of turpentine and linseed oil on a soft cloth. Clean off with hot soapy water and rinse thoroughly after use. Use neat paraffin for the most stubborn stains. Scrub stains from dripping taps with lemon juice, using an old toothbrush dipped in salt. You can also make a paste of borax with white vinegar and brush until it disappears.

To remove limescale on taps, rub vigorously with the cut side of half a lemon. Rinse, and buff dry with a clean soft cloth. To descale tap nozzles, tie a plastic bag filled with vinegar over the nozzle and leave until the scale has dissolved, then rinse. Use an old toothbrush to get rid of the grimy deposits around the base of a tap, using vinegar or lemon juice. To clean chrome taps, rub with a handful of flour, then polish off with a soft cloth. If you have a blocked shower-head, soak it in a bowl of warm vinegar and use a toothbrush or darning needle to clear the holes.

When washing lace curtains, add a spoonful of sugar to the final warm rinse, to keep them crisp. If they become discoloured, soak them in cold tea to dye them a creamy-beige. After washing, hang them while still damp so that they don't shrink – pull them gently into shape.

To neutralize smells in the toilet, strike a match. The smell of the sulphur predominates, and the flame burns away foul-smelling gases. Alternatively, sprinkle a sweet water such as orange-flower water or lavender water (see page 94).

WASTE-NOT-WANT-NOT

From the Garden

If you grow your own herbs, trim them during the summer when they begin to overtake the garden, and dry the trimmings by hanging them upside down in bunches in the kitchen. They add a natural touch, smell lovely, and you can use them for stocks and sauces.

When you have a glut of apples, store them carefully for winter use. I put mine between layers of newspaper, slightly set apart from each other so they are not touching – this slows down the spread of mould. Other people store them in straw. They have to be kept in a cool place like a shed or garage – they go off quickly in a centrally heated house.

If honesty grows in your garden don't weed it out, but pick it in the autumn. Slide off the husks around the beautiful white round heads and use in dried flower arrangements.

Left-over Wallpaper

Use this to line kitchen shelves and chests of drawers. For the larder shelf, cut 4 or 6 layers to size, and remove a layer regularly as it become dirty, so that your storeroom surfaces are always clean.

Keep left-overs to patch any damaged wall areas: cut out a matching piece slightly larger than the area you need to replace, and if you leave the edge slightly irregular the patch will be less noticeable. Glue to the spot, matching the pattern carefully and using a roller to flatten the edges.

Old Toothbrushes

These are incredibly useful for a variety of jobs: cleaning jewellery (see page 15), scrubbing limescale and deposits off taps (see page 15), cleaning grouting (dipped in a solution of bleach) and polishing intricate woodwork or metal work. They get into otherwise inaccessible mouldings on grates, and into the crannies of complicated kitchen equipment.

Good Housekeeping

You can increase the shelf-life of a sponge-mop considerably by storing the sponge end with a plastic bag tied around it to stop it drying out and warping. You can save on detergent when you are washing by adding a tablespoon of bicarbonate of soda to the wash. It also softens the water. And soften dried-out shoe polish with a little turpentine to give it a new lease of life.

Energy-saving Tips

Re-use foil: simply wipe clean with a damp cloth on a flat surface to 'iron' it and prolong its shelf-life. Use it to save energy in the following ways:

Place foil inside a grill pan to reflect heat: not only is this an economy, but it is also useful in that you throw away the foil after use rather than having to scrub grease and other deposits off the pan. You can also economize on heat by placing a sheet of foil under the electric hob. Not only does this reflect heat, it is far easier to keep the stove clean: foil wipes clean easily, burnt objects don't stick, and you simply throw it away when it is heavily soiled, and replace.

Place a sheet of foil under the ironing-board cover to reflect heat into garments.

Plastic Containers

Keep plastic containers (e.g. margarine, yogurt, cottage cheese), and use for freezing food. I put soup into large yogurt containers which conveniently contain one serving. You can also use them as receptacles for cleaning paintbrushes and/or mixing paint.

Linen

Turn old tablecloths into a set of napkins. Make pillowcases from sheets which have worn out in the centre but which are still good around the outsides. Use the un-worn-out parts of flannelette sheeting for children's nighties.

Give sheets a new lease of life by cutting the sheet lengthwise through the centre where it has worn out, or where it tears, and turn the sides to the middle: sew the outer edges together and make a small neat French seam for strength and smoothness. Hem the outer edges. Make single sheets from double sheets, and keep worn-out sheets to use as covers for when you are painting the house, or cut them up and use as polishing cloths.

A needle and thread always come in handy to repair fabric, and can save you a lot of money.

CLEANING

C-l-e-a-n, clean, verb active, to make bright, to scour. W-i-n, wind, d-e-r, der, winder, a casement. When the boy knows this out of the book, he goes and does it. Mr Squeers in *Nicholas Nickleby*, by Charles Dickens

Cleanliness is next to godliness, or so it is said in more than one culture. Let it be observed, that slovenliness is no part of religion, preached John Wesley in the eighteenth century, and Feng Shui has it that clutter, and by implication dirt, blocks the free flow of energy through the home. Certainly a spring-cleaned house is a pleasure, it imparts a sense of the new, of vitality and freshness. Before the days of chemical cleaners our grandmothers used common household or kitchen ingredients to achieve this pristine sparkle: lemons, vinegar, bicarbonate of soda and salt all played a major role, along with the tougher elements of ammonia, methylated spirits, turpentine and white spirit. Borax, glycerine and washing soda have all but been forgotten by the modern housewife, and they are wonderfully effective cleaning agents. Protect your hands by wearing rubber gloves for all these strong substances, to avoid the 'hands like bears' backs' so aptly described by a friend's mother who remembers the days of doing all the family washing by hand. 'What's worth doing is worth doing well', was the adage she repeated often to her daughter. The following tips have been gleaned from people living all over the world, in Singapore, Zimbabwe, Canada and the USA, New Zealand, Iceland and various parts of Europe.

Making home-made beeswax polish.

Housework

The maid of a friend in Singapore always used two dusters while she was cleaning, one in each hand, saying that she would get round in half the time. A good general tip is to soak a new duster in equal parts paraffin and vinegar. Store in a screw-top jar until ready to use, and it will lift out dirt.

Polished Furniture

Use turpentine, an all-purpose solvent, to remove ring marks, rubbing along the grain. A New Zealand friend told me that to remove a watermark on polished furniture, mix a few flicks of cigarette ash with olive oil, rub it in and leave for 30 minutes. Buff with a soft cloth. A mixture of salt and vegetable oil, left on for an hour, also helps remove marks from polished wood. Remove after 30 minutes, then rub with a soft cloth.

To revive dull polish on wooden furniture, mix 2 tablespoons each of turpentine, white vinegar and methylated spirits, which shifts sticky substances, and 1 tablespoon linseed oil, which feeds and protects wood. Shake well, and apply with a soft cloth. For dirty woodwork, mix 1 part turpentine with 1 part vinegar and enough powdered starch to make a paste. Apply with a soft cloth and rub into the grime. Buff with a soft cloth.

Rub linseed oil into lustreless oak to make it shine, and when dusting intricately carved wood use a paintbrush or toothbrush. Remove sticky marks on wood with a little vinegar and water, then apply beeswax, the most nourishing of wax polishes.

Home-made Beeswax Polish

This works beautifully and is far cheaper than buying the polish ready-made.

> *75g (3oz) beeswax*
> *150ml (5fl oz) turpentine*
> *Essential oil of lavender (optional)*

Put the beeswax into a bowl and set it over simmering water until the wax melts. Then add the turpentine and stir thoroughly. Pour into a jar, add a few drops of essential oil of lavender if you wish, and allow to cool.

Other Surfaces

Marble is porous, so treat stains as soon as possible. For wine, coffee or tea stains, use a solution of 1 part white vinegar to 4 parts water. Wipe off at once. Or apply fresh lemon juice to bleach out the stain. You can remove marks on wallpaper by rubbing with a scrunched up piece of white bread, which also works on hessian.

For grease marks on wallpaper, apply a warm iron over brown paper to absorb the grease. Repeat with clean bits of paper until the stain disappears. For rust on metal furniture, simply use a stiff wire brush. To revive dull ebony: rub in petroleum jelly, leave to soak in for 30 minutes, then rub off with a soft cloth.

To clean phones, radios, clock-faces and computer keys, use methylated spirits on cotton wool, and penetrate the inaccessible bits with a cotton-wool bud. Two tablespoons methylated spirits and 2 tablespoons water mixed together will clean dirty piano keys: apply on cotton wool, well squeezed out. Be careful with methylated spirits because it is flammable, but it is useful for removing felt-tip ink and sticky labels.

To clean paintwork, mix 1 tablespoon turpentine, 1 tablespoon milk and 1 tablespoon washing-up liquid with 1.2 litres (2 pints) hot water. Apply with a soft cloth. For scuff marks on vinyl, use an eraser; white spirit or turpentine will also do the job.

Natural Leather Polish for Upholstery

Boil 300ml (½ pint) linseed oil, cool and add 300ml (½ pint) vinegar. Apply with a cloth and then buff to a polish.

Cleaning Bamboo Furniture

From a friend in Germany:

> *1 tablespoon salt*
> *300ml (1pint) water*
> *A little lemon juice (or a mixture of warm water and washing soda)*

Apply with a soft brush into the crevices, and wipe dry with an old piece of velvet soaked in linseed oil. Leave the coating of oil on for an hour or two, then polish off with a soft cloth.

In Singapore they spray cane and bamboo furniture with a plant spray from time to time to keep it supple.

WASHING

'I have no passion for clean linen' growled Dr Samuel Johnson. Many would disagree. In the old days a starch was made from the roots of bluebells and arum lilies, and the crushed leaves of soapwort (*Saponaria officinalis*) produced a home-made soap which produced a good lather. They still do. The presence in the leaves of saponin loosens dirt particles and produces a light lubricating froth, and has been used in modern times by specialists to clean fragile antique fabrics.

Recent rust stains on linen can be removed with cream of tartar mixed to a paste with a little water, spread over the affected area, left to dry and then brushed off. You can also try dabbing on lemon juice, covering with salt and leaving to dry for an hour in the sun if possible. Rinse off, then wash. Soluble aspirin solution will dissolve underarm sweat stains.

If linen gets marked, dip the stain in buttermilk and dry in the sun, then wash in cold water and dry. For iron moulds and mildew: wet the affected part of the cloth and rub with the cut surface of a lemon. My Indian friend uses lime juice to remove ink and other stains from clothes. Beetroot stains are pernicious: rinse

You can use simple, natural treatments on many delicate fabrics.

immediately under cold running water, then soak in a borax solution. Borax is a strong detergent which breaks down grease and softens water at the same time. Wash woollen jumpers and wool jersey outfits inside-out, to prevent matting of the pile, and add a tablespoon of vinegar to the final rinse to revive colours.

Add 1 tablespoon white vinegar – one of the most versatile of home cleaners – to a bowl of rinse water in hand-washing to remove all traces of soap. A teaspoon of Epsom salts added to the last rinse keeps colours bright. Soak well-used flannels (face-cloths) in 1 tablespoon vinegar or lemon juice to 600ml (1 pint) water before machine washing, to remove all traces of soap. Soak cloths in cold water prior to washing, to loosen dirt. To keep colours bright, soak clothes in cold salty water before their first wash.

Special Treatments

When black garments lose their blackness, soak them in water with a little white vinegar, or add water softener to the wash, to remove the build-up of soap that has caused the colour to change. To revitalize black silk, a woman in the village who had worked 'below stairs' in the manor house in the 1920s told me to boil and mash ivy leaves until the water is dark: it acts as a reconditioning dye.

A friend who is one of the few women I know to love housework, and whose home always smells of fresh laundry, gave me these tips: A little methylated spirits added to the rinsing water preserves the sheen of **silk**. Add 2 lumps sugar to the rinse water to give it body, plus a little lanolin to protect and restore it. Sprinkle **lace** with powdered magnesia and leave for a few days before shaking it out – this works like a dry shampoo, the powder absorbing the dirt. To raise the surface of **velvet**, put a wet cloth over a hot iron and hold the velvet over the steam. Brush against the pile with a soft brush and it rises beautifully.

Cleaning the Iron

Clean the base of the iron (unplugged) with toothpaste applied with a soft cloth (unless it is non-stick, in which case you sponge it with a washing-up solution, or use methylated spirits).

Pets in the House

A young puppy can cause havoc with your housework until it is house-trained. Neutralize urine smells on the carpets by making a solution of 1 part vinegar to 5 parts water. Put it into a plant-spray bottle to help remove the smell and deter the animal at the same time. Blot the area with ammonia solution (wearing rubber gloves) to further deter a repetition. Soda water is a useful instant remedy too.

Strips of citrus fruit peel deter cats because they dislike the smell so much – this from a Chinese woman born in Singapore.

Wipe oil of cloves on furniture legs to prevent a new puppy from chewing them – they dislike both the smell and the taste.

For pet hairs on furniture, wrap sticky tape around your fingers, sticky side out, and rub over the upholstery to pick up the hairs.

Carpets

For a 'dry shampoo': sprinkle bicarbonate of soda liberally on to the carpet. It neutralizes acid stains and counteracts smells. Leave for 20–30 minutes, then vacuum off.

Shoe-polish stains can be removed by applying white spirit, a versatile solvent. Allow to dry, then dab out any remaining dye with methylated spirits. Dampen a cloth with turpentine and rub away grease spots then rub softly with a clean cloth to remove traces of the turpentine. Weak vinegar solution is also effective for grease and dirt on carpets. If you find dye stains on the carpet, add a few drops of ammonia to some methylated spirits in a small dish and apply on a cotton pad until the dye vanishes.

If you find cigarette burns on a carpet, rub them with the edge of a silver coin. For beer stains, use the soda syphon, blot well, and clean with bicarbonate of soda (see above). For old beer stains, use methylated spirits. Tea and black coffee also respond to the soda syphon treatment, then sponge with borax solution.

To retrieve tiny objects such as gemstones or contact lenses lost in carpet pile, fit a stocking over the nozzle of the vacuum cleaner and they will be sucked into the fabric.

Windows and Glass

For grimy windows, rub first with the cut side of an onion. Then make a solution of water and vinegar and put into a spray bottle.

A cut onion is useful for cleaning fly specks from glass.

It cuts through grease and brings up a good shine. Then wipe dry newly washed windows with crumpled newspaper – the ink gives a good shine.

For any glass with flyspecks, clean with the cut side of an onion. My old cleaning lady's grandmother useds to boil up 2–3 onions and use the water to remove them. You can also clean up an oil-painting with a cut onion.

Glasses

Add lemon juice to the rinsing water to bring up a shine. For cloudy decanters and vases, mix a handful of salt (or crushed eggshell) with white vinegar and place inside, then fill with washing-up liquid. Shake well and leave for several hours. Rinse thoroughly. Or fill cloudy glasses with water and add 1 teaspoon ammonia to each one. Leave overnight, and wash clean in hot water. For dull glass, make a paste with baking powder and water and rub it in. Wash off and polish with a soft cloth.

For crystal, place 2 teaspoons ammonia inside and fill the vase or decanter with water. Leave to stand for several hours then wash out thoroughly.

If you spill red wine on the carpet, cover the stain with salt (see 'wine' below).

STAINS

The golden rule with stains is to treat them as soon as possible. Laundry borax is excellent, and glycerine helps remove old stains. For example, glycerine mixed into egg white in equal proportions gets old grass stains out of whites. The world's most universal and natural stain remover is the cut side of half a lemon – the acid is a bleaching agent which takes unwanted marks and aromas out.

Stains on Clothes and Upholstery

Blood: soak the fabric in cold water.

Chocolate: sprinkle with borax and soak in cold water before washing.

Coffee: rub fresh stains with glycerine and rinse out with warm water.

Egg: soak in cold water with a little salt added before washing. On furniture, sponge with cold salty water.

Fruit juice: soak in milk for an hour before washing. (This also works for cola stains). Egg stains cutlery black: wipe off deposits and rub the stains with salt applied on a damp cloth.

Grease: A friend told me she smothered her husband's new silk tie in talc after it became heavily stained with cooking grease, and after brushing it off the next day, the staining had disappeared. Rub suede with glycerine to remove grease; and an emery board will restore shiny patches to their original texture.

Hair oil on a headboard: rub with white spirit.

Ink stains on carpets: A woman now in her nineties, who lived in Rhodesia in the 30s, remembers ink being spilled on a pale pink carpet, and the dog proceeding to trot through it. Black South African servants put milk on the stains and they disappeared without trace. You can also rub the stain with the cut side of half a tomato, and rinse out well. Scrub ink stains on the hands with a nailbrush dipped in vinegar and salt. Lemon juice works on this and other dyes left on the hands. For ink stains on wood, dab with neat household bleach on a cotton wool bud and blot with paper towels. When the stain has cleared, apply wax polish.

Mildew: soak in a diluted bleach solution before washing and hang in the sun to dry.

Milk: soak in cold water, then sandwich between kitchen paper and iron out any remaining grease.

Tar: scrape off as much as possible, then treat with eucalyptus oil soaked into a white cloth.

Tea stains on upholstery: sponge with a laundry borax solution.

Wine: sprinkle salt on to a red wine stain on the carpet and leave to absorb, then brush off. Repeat as necesary. Or pour some white wine over it as soon as it happens. Blot well, sponge with clean water and pat dry with kitchen paper. Or use a glycerine solution. On clothes, rinse in warm water, then soak in borax solution (1 tablespoon borax to 600ml/1 pint water) before washing. Old stains may respond to a little methylated spirits on a sponge.

SILVER AND OTHER METALS

For years we lived in a Cambridge College and my mother ran the Master's Lodge with the help of a wonderful couple from St Helena. Here are some of the tips she picked up from them:

Silver: when tarnished, dissolve a handful of washing soda in an aluminium pan, soak the silver in it and remove as soon as the tarnish has disappeared. Rinse and polish. Or use a paste of fine salt and lemon juice. Brighten up silver quickly with a drop of white spirit on a soft cloth.

Brass: clean off heavy tarnish with a solution of vinegar and salt (1 tablespoon salt to 600ml/1 pint vinegar), or washing soda. Clean up with lemon dipped in salt, and rub vigorously. Then wash with warm water and ammonia solution (1 tablespoon ammonia to 600ml/1 pint water). Dry and buff to a polish.

Pewter: mix wood ash to a paste with a little water and rub it in for a dull sheen. Or rub with cabbage leaves. Or immerse in leftover egg-boiling water. Remove grease marks by rubbing with a little methylated spirits on a soft cloth.

Copper: if copper turns green remove the verdigris with a solution of ammonia (see above) using rubber gloves.

Lead: scrub with turpentine or white spirit. If heavily stained, soak for 5 minutes in a solution of 1 part white vinegar to 9 parts water, with a little bicarbonate of soda added.

Brighten up silver instantly with a little white spirit on a soft cloth.

PESTS AND VERMIN

When I was researching a TV series on village life I interviewed a retired gamekeeper and his wife, Lionel and Hilda, who lived in one of the council cottages just outside a pretty village in Hertfordshire. Inside, the house was plain and clean and immaculately tidy – his wife had been a cleaning lady to various villagers all her life. The garden was mostly given over to vegetables, with small borders of annuals around a patch of lawn. The old couple came up with these well-tried methods of pest control in the house, which are largely based on natural eco-friendly methods.

Flies

Beer or treacle in a saucer, or smeared on to sheets of paper, will attract and kill flies. If you are eating out of doors and are plagued by flies and wasps, put down a saucer of jam at a little distance

Thyme is an excellent moth-repellent.

away – it acts as the perfect decoy. Pyrethrum powder (from *Pyrethrum cenerariaefolium*) is an environmentally safe fly-repellent. Scatter it around the windowsills or put on to a plate.

Friends who live in a wonderful house in Pennsylvania surrounded by woodland use the leaves of black walnut (*Juglans nigra*) to keep ants and flies from the house. Rue repels houseflies: Hilda still grows it in a window-box outside the kitchen, and Lionel remembered it being planted as a border next to one of the barns on the farm. If by any mischance you should swallow a fly, Lionel's grandmother's tip was to drink a little vinegar laced with cayenne. This would kill the insect off directly (but goodness knows what it would do to you).

A Frenchwoman living in Morocco showed me her pot of basil by the door: no country home was without one, she declared, because it kept flies out of the house. They are kept in the local bars and shops and living rooms. I immediately tried this on my kitchen windowsill and it substantially reduced the number of flies that plague us during the summer. She also told me that in her house in France she hangs up large bunches of fresh mint in the kitchen to get rid of flies, pinching the leaves every time she passes. I have found that sprigs of wormwood work well too, as well as rue and tansy.

Moths

Take a handful each of dried rosemary, sage and mint, and mix with a little grated lemon peel and a pinch of cinnamon. Tie into muslin bags and lay in drawers or hang in cupboards. Dried wormwood and southernwood are effective moth-repellents too. And if you tie long sprigs of thyme together and hang them in the clothes cupboard they will keep moths away as they dry out.

Fleas

Country tradition has it, according to Hilda, that fleas arrive on March 1st. If you spring-clean that day, early in the morning, the 'black army' will not move in and you will be free from fleas all year. Fleas hate wormwood, and pennyroyal and fennel both repel fleas. Wash your animals in a strong infusion of walnut leaves. Or infuse wormwood overnight and soak the coat thoroughly with the mixture, brush and comb when dry.

A woman on Shelter Island, New York, puts braids of pennyroyal into the dogs' beds to repel fleas and ticks, which they do very effectively. Lionel said that giving your dog an unpeeled garlic clove in its food would repel fleas: it worked immediately on my dog. He also said it would get rid of worms effectively.

Ants

My gardener friend Barbara said to pour boiling water on the nest. Or open it, throw quick-lime over it immediately and throw water over the top. Do the same with the haunts of cockroaches. A friend who lived in the Bahamas for many years used to do what the natives did and scattered pennyroyal over the shelves where the infestation occurred, and the ants were gone in no time. Mint planted by the front door will stop them coming in, so will tansy. The bruised leaves of sprigs of lemon thyme have the same effect, and all these are much pleasanter than the toxic substances that you may buy. In the larder, hang pennyroyal, rue or tansy, and sprinkle chilli powder on the shelves when they appear. Mineke, who comes from West Friesland north of Amsterdam, remembers her mother drawing a chalk line across the threshold to stop ants coming into the house. It worked!

Cockroaches

A friend in New York City has found that the best roach repellent is to put down an equal mix of bicarbonate of soda or borax and icing sugar. It's the borax that gets them. A traditional country poison is the black hellebore which grows on marshland. Strew it on the floor: the cockroaches will eat it when they come out at night and will be found dead or dying the next morning.

For crickets and beetles, place scotch snuff or chloride of lime in the holes which they frequent.

Mice

Leaves of dwarf elder (*Sambucus ebulus*) drive mice away from stored grain. Vetchling or everlasting sweet pea (*Lathyrus latifolius*) repels field mice and other small rodents, and spearmint planted near the house has the reputation of keeping rodents away. The spurges (*Euphorbia lathyrus* and *E. lactea*) repel moles and mice.

The arch pest controller …

An old gentleman in his nineties had a father and grandfather who had both worked as book-keepers. They added powdered wormwood (*Artemesia absinthinium*) to the ink which they used for writing out their figures, and this stopped mice and rats eating the ledgers.

'Get a cat', said Lionel.

Rats

Make a thick paste with 1.5kg (3lb) flour and water to mix. Dissolve 25g (1oz) phosphorus and 50g (2oz) turmeric in 40g (1½oz) butter and mix in. Spread this on to bread where the rats can get it, or make into balls, rolled in sugar. Or you can impregnate hay with cayenne pepper and stuff it down their holes and they are unlikely to pass through the barrier. Simply sprinkling cayenne down their holes is unpopular enough and 'will certainly send them off at a sneezing pace'.

'Get a terrier', said Lionel.

Spiders

The final word comes from a grandmother who said that when big hairy spiders come in to the house it means autumn is coming, and they must be left alone. She used to call them 'the charladies'

FIREPLACES

Where glowing embers through the room
Teach light to counterfeit a gloom,
Far from all resort of mirth,
Save the cricket on the heart.

John Milton, *L'Allegro* (1632)

There is a brick jutting out near the top of the chimney in my three-hundred-year-old thatched cottage, and I am told this was called the witches' seat, provided for her so that she would not come down any further. The inglenook has a small cavity in the wall which was used to store the household salt, to keep it dry. Witches hate salt, so I have double protection. One old builder told me they used to put salt-glazed bricks into the chimney to keep them away. Be that as it may, an open fireplace is the heart of the house, a place to gather and gaze into the flames and talk and listen to stories and roast chestnuts. A woman now in her eighties, who used to work as a maid in a stately home in Oxfordshire, was told that the fireplace must be kept spotlessly clean because it was the 'altar of the house'.

Firewood

My German friend Inge was told by her grandfather never to burn elder wood in the house: it was very unlucky because the wood spits and could cause a fire, and anyway it brings the Devil down the chimney. Ash is the best wood – it burns hot and long, and doesn't spit. Pine is dangerous because it sends out showers of sparks so never be tempted to burn up bits of old pine furniture. Cut your wood in the summer and let it 'season' or dry out – wood should not be burned while the sap is running as all it does is hiss at you from the grate. Also, well-seasoned wood is less

A log fire burning in the hearth is the heart of the home.

likely to spark. Keep your wood supply under cover to prevent rain and snow falling on it. If you don't have a wood shed, stack it under a sheet of plastic, allowing air to circulate from the sides.

If you have a large fireplace and need a lot of kindling to start the fire, tie it in a bundle with a twist of pliant twig (not string, which burns immediately) so that the heart of the fire does not collapse. To add fragrance to the fire, throw citrus peel on to it, or pine cones which are beautifully aromatic. If you burn hickory wood it will fill the house with its aroma, and apple wood smells fabulous. You can make good use of wood ash: put ashes on the driveway to make a hard core – it packs down gradually. Or put it on to the garden or the compost heap (see page 51).

Soot Marks

Salt helps shift soot marks from the carpets – just sprinkle it over and brush clean. Talcum powder is good too. For soot marks on brickwork surrounding the fire, use a stiff bristle – or even wire – brush dipped in a warm water-vinegar solution. Or rub with a another piece of brick. Thick residues of soot may have to be chiselled off. Use neat vinegar for scorch marks. On stonework, use washing-up liquid solution, and add a bit of bleach if necessary.

Cleaning the Chimney

An old-fashioned way of sweeping the chimney over a wood fire was to drop one end of rope with a big bunch of holly leaves tied halfway along it, big enough to thoroughly scrape the edges, down the chimney. You have one person at each end and work up and down until the chimney is cleaned of excess soot.

Toasting Goodies by the Fireside

Get yourself a toasting fork and make toast, holding the bread at a judicious distance from the flame so as not to burn it. Likewise with marshmallows: just get them hot enough and near enough to the flame to give them a crust all over the outside, then remove, cool a little and you will find the inside gooey. You can even try an impromptu 'fondue', putting 2cm (¾in) cubes of cheese on to the toasting fork, turning them in the flame until they begin to melt. This takes practise: it is easy to overcook and lose the whole thing with a hiss as it disappears into the flames. When you succeed

Toasting marshmallows on a winter's evening.

however, the smoky flavour and the melting texture are fabulous. But beware of putting anything cooked like this straight into your mouth – you could be horribly burned by the hot metal of the fork. Always remove the hot article on to a plate first, to cool a little before you eat it.

If you have a big wood fire with a lot of hot ash underneath, bake potatoes there by smothering them and leaving to cook in the hot ashes for about an hour. Best of all on winter nights are roasted chestnuts: wait until the fire dies down, slit the tops of the chestnuts which otherwise will explode violently, and put into the hot embers. Leave for 5–7 minutes before picking put carefully with tongs. Alternatively, use a chestnut roaster, an iron holder with holes in, on a long handle. Hold it over the fire for 5–7 minutes, then allow to cool slightly before you peel them.

If you put a candle in the freezer for a few hours, it burns for longer.

CANDLES

Absence diminishes commonplace passions and increases great ones,
as the wind extinguishes candles and kindles fire.
Duc de la Rochfoucauld (1613–80)

Candles were invented in the ancient world, as evidenced by Egyptian and Cretan candlesticks dating back to 3000BC. There is a legend that King Alfred the Great (849–899) used candles to measure the passing of time. Placed in a lantern to protect them from draughts, each one would burn for four hours. By 1272 there were seventy-one chandlers or candlemakers working in Paris, according to a tax list.

The soft light of a candle brings beauty to a room and is flattering to the skin, but its romantic connotations are not without risks: 'Choose neither women nor linen by candlelight', says country wisdom. Nowadays there are floating candles, scented candles, and candles of many colours and shapes for creating atmosphere within the home. Modern candles are a composite of paraffin and stearic acid, sometimes with beeswax or bayberry wax added.

Candles have been used in religious and spiritual ceremonies and rituals all over the world for centuries. The Roman Catholic Church used to stipulate that candles were 100 per cent pure beeswax, but now the measure is down to only 25 per cent. There was a tenth-century Welsh law that stated that a Mass could only be said when bees were present – in the form of beeswax candles. Bees are holy because they swarmed out of Paradise in disgust at the Fall of Man.

The obvious analogy of lighting the darkness made candles symbols for purity and enlightenment:

I shall light a candle of understanding in thine heart, which shall not be put out. Esdras VIII.25

Practical Tips

Place new candles in the freezer for a few hours to make them burn longer. Dip a candle end in very hot water to soften it before putting into a candlestick: heating it with a match marks it black. If the holder is loose, wrap the end of the candle in adhesive tape.

Removing wax from pewter candlesticks: place them in the freezer for an hour or two, then the wax peels off easily. Use a hairdryer to melt away any remaining wax. On china candlesticks, remove the excess with a blunt knife, then place in the microwave on full power for 1–2 minutes to soften the remaining wax, which you can then rub off easily with your fingertips. Silver candlesticks: pour hot water over the candlestick to remove the wax. Melt the remainder with a hairdryer.

Cleaning up candlewax on a wood floor: let it harden (speed this up with an ice cube), then ease off with a blunt knife, rub in some polish and buff with a soft cloth.

Allow spilt wax on the carpet to harden. Gently scrape off what you can without damaging the pile. Then set the iron to warm and blot the rest of the wax through absorbent kitchen paper and keep changing it until all traces of wax have disappeared.

On clothes, treat with methylated spirits which will also absorb colour dye. On wallpaper and furniture, use the paper technique.

To Make a Rush Candle

Rushlights were once the most economical source of domestic lighting for rural homes. Here is an old-fashioned recipe for making a rush taper, from the days when chandling was a home craft. It would be mounted on to a piece of tree bark and lit to give a soft light after dark. The great advantage of rush lights is that they do not drip.

Cut soft rushes (*Juncus effusus* or *J. conglomeratus*) when they are fully grown but still green. Cut off both ends, peel the green skin and hang up to dry.

Melt some grease – mutton is best, or the grease obtained from boiling marrow bones. Add beeswax to make it burn extra bright. Soak the rushes in the grease and take them out to dry hard. Do this several times until well coated.

Superstitions and Sayings

Candles have given rise to many common sayings: 'to hold a candle to the devil' is to assist an evil person. If the 'game is not worth the candle', the enterprise is not worth the labour or expenditure. To 'burn the candle at both ends' is to be excessively wasteful or extravagant. To be 'not fit to hold a candle' means not to be compared with.

It is unlucky to light a candle from the fire on the hearth. The accumulation of wax dripping to one side of a candle foretells death, because it looks like a shroud. To snuff a candle accidentally is a portent of a wedding. An actor friend told me that three candles in the dressing-room, or on the stage, bring bad luck.

How far that little candle throws its beams!
So shines a good deed in a naughty world.
William Shakespeare *The Merchant of Venice* (1596–7)

The soft light fom candles is flattering to the skin.

COMMON SUPERSTITIONS

Most cultures have invented superstions as a kind of accessible everyday magic to protect against unseen forces. This magic is distinctive to its own society but may also find echoes in another, however distant.

Household

'Touch wood' is said to have come from the old days when relics of the True Cross were kept in churches and solemn oaths were sworn on them. The wrought iron S and X shapes on cottage walls have a superstition behind their obvious practical use: they act as lightning conductors as well as wall props, but the S represents the thunderbolt of Jupiter, the X or swastika the hammer of Thor. Acorns used to be hung at the window to protect the house from lightning, and window-blind pulls are still today fashioned as acorns: the sacred nature of the oak, Jupiter's tree, brought into the home. Everyone knows that horseshoes are lucky, but remember that they should be nailed upwards, and with their own nails. Upside down, all the good luck spills out. Breakages always come in threes, according to many.

Never hang a garment on a doorknob, my neighbour told me, because they used to hang a piece of clothing on the outer knob of the door to tell you that someone inside had died. Never open an umbrella in the house, said a man from Minnesota. Spilling salt is unlucky: to reverse this you must immediately throw some over your left shoulder. My Dutch friend, Mineke, was told that if you dropped butter on the floor it meant you would have a visitor.

Spiders

Spiders have long been supposed to bring good luck and prosperity:

> If you wish to live and thrive
> Let the spider run alive.

One legend goes that during the Flight into Egypt Joseph hid the Holy Family in a cave and a spider wove a web across the entrance. Seeing it unbroken, the pursuing soldiers concluded that no one had entered.

A young woman who lived on Tahiti for a while told me that there spiders are sacred because they are thought to be 'shadows of the gods', and to kill one was extremely unlucky.

Mirrors

Breaking a mirror means seven years bad luck. But if you wash the broken bits in the stream, or bury them, you reverse the curse.

Primitive man believed that his reflection was that of his soul, and if anything separated it from his body – by breaking the mirror for example – he would die. Something dreadful would happen if you looked in a mirror where a dead person lies because you will see the reflection of the deceased looking over your shoulder. So a custom arose of veiling the mirror. If you look into a mirror and see no reflection that is the worst of all: death is certain, for the soul has already departed. Napoleon believed these superstitions and during a campaign in Italy he broke the glass over a miniature of Josephine that he carried with him. He could not sleep until the courier returned assuring him that no ill had befallen his beloved.

My Russian friend Olga used to love looking at her distorted reflection in the curves of her grandmother's shiny teapot. Grandmother would take the pot away saying: 'Never look at yourself in a mirror at table – it will eat up your beauty!'

Cats

A local thatcher told me that his grandfather used to put a dead cat into the thatch as he worked, to protect the house from evil spirits and fire.

A three-hundred-year-old mummified cat – buried alive in the brickwork of a fireplace to ward off evil spirits – was found in the Mill Hotel in Sudbury in Suffolk by builders doing renovations. They tossed the gruesome object into the skip. Over the next four years the mill's foundations started to subside, its fabric to crumble, and a major fire broke out. The builder, knowing something about cat superstitions, had not dared throw the cat away, and the manager persuaded him to retrieve it from his yard. It is now restored to pride of place in a glass case in the hotel entrance and no further harm has come to the building.

LOVE LORE

Gather the Rose of love, whilst yet is time,
Whilst loving thou mayst loved be with equal crime.
Edmund Spenser, *The Faerie Queene*, (1596)

Around the world love lore centres on aphrodisiacs, some less grounded in fancy than others. The most famous, rhino horn, is aphrodisiac by sympathetic magic only, not for any special chemistry, but because of its hardness. Whereas ambergris, taken from the intestine of the sperm whale, has a strong musky smell which is a turn-on and has been used for centuries to oil the path of love (or lust). Hippocrates claimed that ass's meat with milk and honey was aphrodisiac, and until not so long ago it was fed to the harems of Istanbul to keep up their stamina. Brides in the Balkans used to have their faces smeared with honey, which is thought to be aphrodisiac – indeed so much so that the Magyars smeared the sex organs of young men and women with honey to ensure their mutual attraction.

St Valentine's Day, February 14th, is and has been since time immemorial the moment to choose a sweetheart and exchange gifts, although the saint himself is obscure and seems to have no connection with romance other than dying for his faith. Chaucer in *The Parlement of Foules* refers to a belief that birds choose their mates on this day.

When I was visiting Sicily I was introduced to an Italian woman who told me of a most bizarre match-making custom. Her grandmother had saved her mother's umbilical cord. Over the years it dried out; but when the time came to make a good match for her daughter she had powdered it into the cake and wine that she gave to the man she wished her daughter to marry. The idea was that the man would be so overcome with love that he would propose marriage immediately.

Some Aphrodisiacs

Absinthe

Contains absinthine and thujone – which is also found in vermouth in small amounts – and these have an aphrodisiac effect.

Banana

Contains the alkaloid bufotenine in its skin which is a hallucinogen found in some magic mushrooms (and the skins of toads so beloved by witches).

Jamaican Banana Power

Fill a baking dish with ripe bananas, slit the skins lengthwise and bake at 180°C/350°F/gas 4 for 20 minutes. Carefully remove the cooked fruit from the skins. Scoop out the inner linings of the skins with the juices, mix these with rum and pour over the fruit with a sprinkling of allspice. Serve with cream . . . and so to bed.

Cocoa

Waxy beans from the cocoa pod contain phenelethylamine, a mood-altering chemical with orgasmic effect. Aztecs brought cocoa food for the gods for this reason and used it as an aphrodisiac. Montezuma would drink 50 cups a day and make love to as many women. Cocoa was introduced into Europe by the returning Conquistadores in the sixteenth century, and today's researchers, find that it is a mild genital tonic due to its diuretic action. (But huge amounts are required.)

Chestnut Blossom

Contains a combination of chemicals also found in the seminal secretions of the male. Socrates taught the young men of Athens under a chestnut tree, and the Marquis de Sade noted its aphrodisiac effect. You can use the blossoms in sachets or soak them in the bath water (see page 92).

Herbs

Coriander's lovely scent and flavour is so pleasing to the senses that when brewed with honey and water it qualified to the Crusaders as a love potion. Ginger, a 'hot' herb, enhances sexual excitement. Rocket used to be banned from monasteries in France and England because it 'excited the games of love'.

'But alas! There are no herbs to cure love' Ovid

Angel Water

An eighteenth-century English recipe suggests using rose-water, myrtle water and orange-blossom water, some distilled spirit of musk and a dash of ambergris. This was often presented to the happy couple at country weddings to get the couple off to a flying start.

There are hundreds of superstitions and divinations in love lore, enough to fill books. I was brought up with – among others:

Monday for wealth
Tuesday for health
Wednesday best day of all
Thursday for losses
Friday for crosses
Saturday no luck at all.

It was advice I failed to hear: a doomed marriage took place on a Thursday.

If you change the name and not the letter
You marry for worse and not for better

turned out in my case to be true. I should have listened. It coincided with another warning:

Marry in Lent
Live to repent.

I did.

In India, arranged Hindu marriages will only go ahead if the horoscopes match: the art of synastry is practised on the two charts. If a very rich man wants a particular daughter-in-law and knows that the stars don't work he will bribe the astrologer to get his way.

Some Love Proverbs

A maid that laughs is half taken.
Love is like linen, often changed, the sweeter.
A woman that cries hush, bids kiss.
A woman kissed is half won.

Frosted holly leaves make an unusually pretty cake decoration.

FESTIVALS IN THE HOME

The great religious festivals of the world bring families and communities together to perform traditional rituals, often residues of pagan ones, which include feasting. The bonding effect of these events makes it an important time for the family, in whichever part of the world. For Diwali, India's festival of Light, small earthenware lamps are filled with oil, placed in their temples and houses, and set adrift on rivers and streams. At the Jewish Passover, bitter herbs are eaten symbolizing the harsh life of the Hebrews under the Egyptian yoke. Nowadays, celery, romaine lettuce, parsley, chicory and horseradish root are served. The Chinese celebrate their New Year with colourful pageantry and feasting, the Mexicans their Day of the Dead, the Druids the Summer Solstice, the Irish

St Patrick's Day. Easter is a major festival in the Christian world, whereas the Japanese celebrate the Buddha's birthday at Kambutsue. And so on: human beings love to celebrate, and no more so than at Christmas and Thanksgiving.

Many people feel that Christmas is over-commercialized. But you can still make your own cards and decorations and wreaths – I shall never forget one beautiful wreath made by an American friend with the evergreen herbs rosemary, thyme, rue, winter savory and sweet laurel. Certainly your own home-made food, made in the tradition of our mothers and grandmothers, gives Christmas that personal touch and family feel: this tiny selection gives a flavour of the charm of an old-fashioned Christmas.

Christmas

Frosted Holly Leaves

This old-fashioned and very pretty notion was given to me by a lady approaching her hundredth birthday, who told me that she remembered her grandmother making them, for decorating the Christmas cake.

Pick the leaves from their stalks and wipe them clean and dry. Hang up in the airing cupboard to dry for 2 days. Then dip them first into melted butter and then into caster sugar and put them on to a tray. Return them to the airing cupboard or over the boiler to dry for a further 2 days.

Cranberry Rope

This Christmas decoration using cranberries was described to me by a woman living in New York City who remembered picking them as a child in the bogs near her home in Massachusetts.

Pick the cranberries and clean them. Thread a medium needle with waxed thread and thread the cranberries carefully on to it, making the rope as long as you need. You can also alternate the berries with popcorn to make a red and white rope. The berries dry out over the days and end up like beads, and of course they shrink which makes the rope shorter – so allow for this by making it extra-long. The occupational hazard of this is that your hands get stained red (remove the stain with lemon juice, see page 22).

This rope looks extremely pretty twisted around the light wires on the tree.

Christmas Cookies

These are the Proustian madeleines of my life. My American mother used to make 'sugar cookies' as she called them and they are an integral part of childhood, bringing distant memories into focus.

MAKES 24	100g (4oz) butter
100g (4oz) plain flour	Grated zest of half a lemon
100g (4oz) granulated sugar	2 teaspoons vanilla

Preheat the oven to 180°C/350°F/gas 4.

Mix the flour with the sugar and rub in the butter until it is like very fine breadcrumbs, then add the lemon zest and vanilla. Knead on a wooden board to a soft dough. If you want them to hold their shape, add a little more flour (a scant 15g /½oz) to make a stiffer dough.

Roll out fairly thinly and cut into rounds or other shapes – either make up your own and do them freehand, or use cutter shapes (stars, trees, angels, etc.) If you are going to hang them on the tree, puncture a small hole near the top edge before baking. Bake for 8–10 minutes, until a light golden colour. Allow to cool for 3–4 minutes, then lift off carefully and cool on a wire rack.

Luxury Wassail Cup (see also page 169)

This celebratory cup for Christmas is steeped in tradition. If you are pouring the hot liquid straight into glasses, put a metal spoon in first to conduct the heat so that the glass doesn't break in your hand.

SERVES 15	4 bottles port, sherry or Madeira
Scant 7g (¼oz) whole cardamoms,	675g (1 ½lb) sugar
cloves, nutmeg, mace, ginger,	12 egg yolks and 6 whites
cinnamon and coriander	12 apples, baked until they burst

Simmer the spices in a little water, covered, for 15 minutes. Strain into the wine, add the sugar and dissolve over a low heat. Leave on a low heat for 30 minutes, not allowing it to boil. Beat the eggs in a large bowl and pour over a cupful of the hot wine, beating well. Gradually add the remainder of the wine, whisking all the time until frothy.

Add the apples, which will float like froth on the top, and serve.

Thanksgiving

The North American tradition of Thanksgiving goes back to the autumn of 1621 when the Massachusetts Bay Governor William Bradford invited neighbouring Indians to join the pilgrims for a three-day feast in gratitude for the harvest and the blessings of the past year. It caught on. Thanksgiving Day was proclaimed a national holiday by Abraham Lincoln in 1863, and Canada adopted it in 1879. Roast turkey, cranberry sauce and pumpkin pie are the order of the day.

Stuffed Acorn Squash

A wonderful dish to serve up alongside the roast turkey and cranberry sauce.

SERVES 8–10

2.25kg (5lb) acorn squash

STUFFING

100g (4oz) wild rice

1 teaspoon salt

175g (6oz) mushrooms, chopped finely

25g (1oz) butter

50g (2oz) red onion, chopped finely

50g (2oz) cheese, grated

2 teaspoons ground ginger

Salt and pepper

100g (4oz) brown breadcrumbs

3 tablespoons olive oil

Preheat the oven to 200°C/400°F/gas 6. Put the squash on to a baking sheet and bake for 50–60 minutes, until a sharp knife inserted into the centre goes in easily and all the flesh is soft. Cool, then make a cut horizontally and scrape out the seeds and fibres.

Cook the wild rice for 30 minutes in boiling water, or until tender, adding the salt during the last 5 minutes. Cook the mushrooms and onion in the butter for 4–5 minutes until softened. Mix into the cooked wild rice with the cheese and ginger and season to taste. Preheat the oven to 180°C/350°F/gas 4.

Pile the filling into the cavities of the squash. Crisp the breadcrumbs in the olive oil, tossing until coated all over. Sprinkle the squash with the crumbs and bake in the bottom of the oven (to prevent the crumbs burning) for 35–40 minutes.

Old-fashioned Cranberry Sauce

This recipe was given to me by the grandmother of a large family who has been making this sauce since the 1940s. She used to make it with canned cranberries, I used fresh: take your pick. It is absolutely brilliant, and it freezes well. You've got enough to do what with all the rest of the food so the simplicity of this labour-saving recipe is a godsend.

225g (8oz) cranberries, canned, fresh or frozen

300g (10oz) mandarin orange sections from a can, with juices

75g (3oz) granulated sugar

50g (2oz) walnut pieces

Simmer the cranberries with the mandarins and their juices, the sugar and the walnuts until they are mushy, about 5 minutes. Then crush lightly with a potato masher, and the sauce is ready to serve.

Pecan Pumpkin Pie

A great finale to the feast. This is the best recipe I've ever tasted for pumpkin pie: it will dispel all doubts that non-Americans may have about this delicacy. It is scrumptious, light and mouthwatering with its creamy, golden filling and the crunch of nuts on top. You will find it unforgettable.

225g (8oz) shortcrust pastry

450g (1lb) slice of pumpkin, deseeded

150ml (¼ pint) single cream

3 eggs, lightly beaten

175g (6oz) brown sugar

2 teaspoons cinnamon

½ teaspoon each allspice, ginger and nutmeg

Pinch of salt

2–3 tablespoons brandy (optional)

50g (2oz) pecan halves

Preheat the oven to 170°C/325°F/gas 3. Roll out the pastry and use to line a 23cm (9in) flan tin. Line the pastry with foil, fill with baking beans and bake blind for 20 minutes. Remove the foil and leave to cool.

Preheat the oven to 200°C/400°F/gas 6. Wrap the pumpkin in foil and bake for 25–30 minutes until tender. Cool, then remove the skin. Blend to a purée in the food processor, and add the cream. Beat the eggs with the sugar and spices until they are thick, and fold in. Flavour with brandy and pour into the prepared pie shell. Decorate the top with the pecan halves. Leave the oven at the same temperature as before.

Bake the pie for 40 minutes, or until a knife inserted into the centre comes out clean. Cool on a wire rack and eat warm, served with thick cream and followed by a cup of the best coffee.

Originally, Thanksgiving was celebrated on the last Thursday in November, but in 1941 it was set on the fourth Thursday of that month. The Canadians celebrate it on the second Monday in October. Thanksgiving brings families together around the traditional food-laden table. Eating, drinking and talking take up most of the day and old bonds are renewed in an atmosphere of feasting and celebration.

GARDENING MAGIC

The gardener half artist must depend
On that slight chance, that touch beyond control
Which all his paper planning will transcend;
He knows the means but cannot rule his end;
He makes the body: who supplies the soul?
Vita Sackville West, *The Garden* (1946)

From earliest civilization mankind has engaged in the engrossing activity of cultivating a small enclosed piece of ground called a garden: a personal paradise – a green thought in a green shade – to fulfil practical or aesthetic needs, or both. From sacred groves and a vision of an archetypal Eden have evolved flower and fruit gardens, kitchen gardens, rose gardens, pleasure gardens, landscape gardens. As men and women planted and toiled, knowing success and failure, a vast tradition of gardening wisdom both oral and written began to grow. It is immense, international and universal.

I have gleaned some of this traditional wisdom by talking with many gardeners who have contributed their commonsense experience to this book. Other knowledge I picked up in childhood from my mother's gardener Mr Williams, who became my personal archetype. He worked for us for many years, and our garden was to me the magical place of childhood. I loved to trail around after him, watch what he did and pester him with questions. His way of speaking and turn of phrase are lodged in my memory. He seemed very old indeed to me then, a tall stooping man who always wore a cap and an old tweed jacket. He was forever dropping wise remarks about the wind or the weather, the phases of the moon or which plants to put next to which, all of which he had learned from his grandfather. Most of it went over my head then, but as I started to tend a garden myself much of it resurfaced, and it appears here in its inherited version.

Making a selection of the country wisdom of the garden is a well-nigh impossible task. Enough books to fill libraries have been written through the ages on such fascinating topics as divining weather, planting at the correct phase of the moon, enriching the soil with compost, companion planting, the work of bees and butterflies, the curse of insect pests, and the microlife of a garden. Likewise, the folklore of flowers and trees, steeped as it is in a fascinating mixture of science and superstition, is impressive in its immensity. A few pages can claim only to give the reader a taste of this universal practical wisdom with its delicate touches of fantasy.

Red sky at night, Shepherd's delight

WEATHER LORE

Those that are weather-wise
Are rarely otherwise

So Mr Williams, my mother's gardener, used to observe. Although much traditional weather lore is unsubstantiated, it is still widely believed, and in many cases meteorological science has not come up with anything better. Man has always sought to control or predict the weather, in an eternal attempt to understand and come to terms with the environment. It is in the temperate countries, where the climate is most variable and the seasons least dependable, where weather lore has flourished: it is relatively rare in the tropics and sub-tropics where the climate is more stable.

The roots of weather lore lie in early religion. Its first exponents were priests or wise men who decided the all-important dates of sowing or harvest. Fertility of the crops, on which survival depended, meant the accurate interpretation of weather signs. Sailors and navigators became adept at this,

because failure could lead to certain death, so much of their lore is reliable. For example, an oncoming gale can set up a rolling swell which travels rapidly ahead, giving warning of bad weather to come before any other indicators such as cloud or rain.

Fine Weather

Year after year I remember Mr Williams saying the weather would be fine if swallows, martins or skylarks flew high, and he never tired of repeating: 'Red sky at night, shepherd's delight.' A friend who lives in northern California quotes this version: 'Red sky at night, sailor's delight.'

Common as this saying is in its various forms, it is not always trustworthy, although the next part of it, just as widespread – 'Red sky at morning, shepherd's [sailor's] warning' – is found in various forms throughout the world and reflects a scientific reality: the scattering of light rays linked to thermal stratification or the formation of atmospheric currents. It is generally accepted as a reliable piece of weather lore.

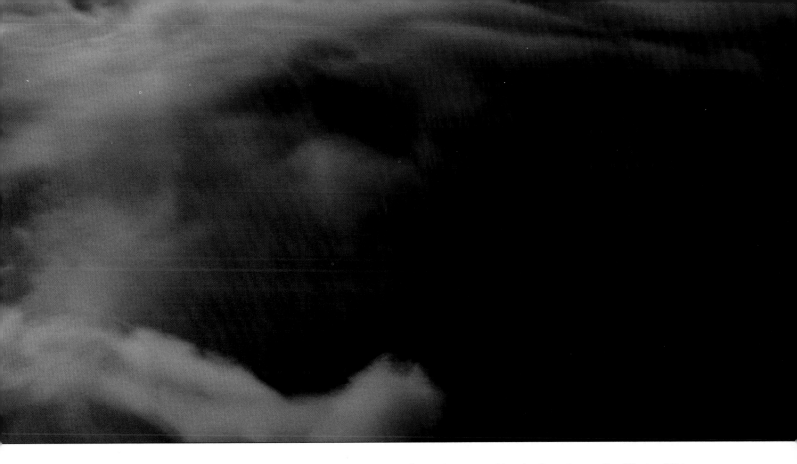

Clouds and Wind

Clouds may indicate weather changes: 'Mackerel sky, twelve hours dry.' My neighbour used to call it a 'cruddly' sky: in meteorological terms this sky, dappled with small white fleecy clouds, is a cirrocumulus formation marking the end of unsettled weather. Looking at the movement of upper layers of clouds can tell you if a change of weather is imminent, if their direction is very different from the winds blowing clouds below. A Moroccan woman told me a famous legend that locusts know where it will rain in the Sahara. In fact, swarms fly downwind until they meet an area of convergent winds, where rain is most likely.

Virgil said that 'rain and wind increase after a thunderclap', and this appears to be borne out as an accurate observation throughout the centuries. The Zuni Indians of New Mexico had a saying that: 'If the first thunder is from the east, winter is over', also grounded in generations of experience and found to be true. But probably the best guide to weather prediction, grounded in careful observation by men and women close to the cycles of nature, is in the wind. Francis Bacon said that: 'Every wind has its weather', a belief shared by many cultures, from the ancient Greeks to the American Indians. 'Do business with men when the wind in in the north-west', goes an old saying from the north of England. This wind, usually accompanied by a rising barometer, has been shown to be related to such diverse events as increased activity on the New York Stock Exchange, and a greater success rate in the artificial insemination of ewes in France!

Looking at the movement of clouds can tell you if a change of weather is imminent.

Rain

Many persistent country sayings about the weather are not grounded in science, but they have not been disproved either. If ants retreat into their burrows, rain will not be far behind. If a candle will not light easily, it means rain; a wavering flame means windy weather is on the way. If the down flies off dandelions, coltsfoot or thistles when there is no wind, it is a sign of rain. 'Rain from the east, two wet days at least'. These are mere observations, but they may contain some truth. An Irish musician told me that the call of a curlew predicts a downpour, and that horses get restless and shake their heads just before rain. One of the most prevalent beliefs is that it will rain if cattle lie down in the fields. Possibly cattle have learned, and passed on through their genes as an adaptive process, to find a dry spot before it is too late. The most that can be said is that animals do indeed behave in particular ways under certain meteorological conditions, and so can be said to provide a forecast of kinds. Bees fly home if bad weather is coming. Many insects hatch in the humid weather before a storm, and swallows fly low to catch them. Owls hoot more at night, and cocks crow more frequently when there is rain about.

My German friend Inge's grandfather worked on the land all his life. He swore that he could predict rain by his corns and rheumatism. Widespread as this lore is, there is no evidence to prove the connection. Men, like plants and animals, react quickly to climate, but other factors such as diet, temperament and anxiety levels also have to be taken into account.

An old lady from deepest Herefordshire told me that in her experience beetles always come out of their haunts before rain, and worms too, presumably to escape drowning. On the other hand: 'Fine weather next day if bats or beetles fly late in the evening' is a common country saying in East Anglia. My friends from Oregon mentioned trees such as poplar and silver maple turning up their leaves when it starts to rain, an observation well known in Europe also. Scientists now know that plants react quickly to their environment, and their survival depends on the genetic transmission of safety responses, so they can be read as consistent weather indicators.

I was brought up with the dictum from my American mother: 'rain before seven, dry before eleven', and learned early to distinguish a rain cloud – the cumulus cloud:

A round-topped cloud with a flattened base
Carries rainfall in its face.

Many people, myself included, take a rain check on St Swithin's Day (July 15th): 'If it do rain, for forty days it will remain.' This piece of lore has entered commonplace wisdom, based on long-term observations and passed on down through generations. Science has not been able to either prove or disprove it. Likewise with this well-known piece of country weather lore which Wilf, my beekeeper neighbour, used to come out with every year:

If the oak's before the ash
There will only be a splash
If the ash before the oak
Then we're sure to get a soak.

'Rain before seven, dry before eleven!'

The moon is an enduring focus of weather lore.

The Moon

The moon features large in weather lore, in spite of the absence of scientific explanation. The nearest is the 'ring around the moon', a white halo sometimes tinged with red, formed by refraction through ice crystals in the clouds and often seen when rain is approaching. It is not however infallible. A woman from Oregon told of her mother's dictum that a ring around the moon means rain next day – a well-known saying all over the world:

> If the moon shows like a silver shield
> You needn't be afraid to reap your field;
> But if she rises haloed round,
> Soon we'll tread on deluged ground.

Some country folk say that a new moon brings a change in the weather, that sharp horns mean windy weather, and that the full moon clears the sky and brings good weather:

> The moon on its back
> Holds rain in its lap

Emanuele, living in rural France near Vaugines, has noted that when the weather turns bad at the start of the new moon, it will stay bad for the whole lunar cycle.

Cold Weather

When I was a child my best friend's grandfather always used to say: 'If the cat turns her back on the fire there will be frost', while my old neighbour Wilf, in his best Essex dialect, used to say: 'An east wind is a lazy one; it will go through you before it goes round you.' These signs were immutable: if nuts or berries hang on the branches after leaf fall, it means a hard winter ahead: 'Many haws, many sloes, many cold toes' and 'When the oak wears his leaves in October you can expect a hard winter.'

> Holly berries shining red
> Mean a long winter, 'tis said.

There is always one fine week in February in England, or later if winter is late, but beware the 'blackthorn hatch'. This warm weather brings the sloe into blossom, but spring is not just around the corner: it is immediately followed by a patch of very severe weather. Ever since Wilf, sadly now departed, told me this, I have observed it happen unfailingly each year.

We all know that if March comes in like a lion, it goes out like a lamb and vice versa. And 'cast not a clout till May be out' because 'in the middle of May comes the tail of winter', according to the wise.

'Sow seeds in the afternoon', they say, 'as the earth draws in'.

PLANTING WISDOM

The phases of the moon are closely associated with fertility, and their importance in planting lore occurs so often all over the world that it is hard to dismiss them as superstition.

The Moon

Traditional wisdom has it that the time when you put the seed into the ground is of utmost importance for its success: root crops should be sown when the moon is waning, while a new moon is auspicious for crops that grow above ground, so that the waxing moon influences them. I am convinced that there is more than something in this, so is an Indian friend who has the greenest fingers of anyone I know.

'Sow corn when the moon is waxing, never when it is waning' goes an English saying. The exception is watery plants such as

marrows, cucumbers and courgettes, which are best sown at full moon. A gardener in Shropshire who had worked the land all his life quoted this:

> *Cut all things or gather, the moon in the wane,*
> *But sow in increasing, or give it its bane.*

The mother of an Indian friend who lives in Jaipur told me that onions are much larger and better nourished if sown during a waning moon. She also said to plant potatoes with a rising tide so they grow with it, and to sow all kinds of pulses with the moon in Cancer.

A Dutch friend's grandmother has a saying: 'Trees are not to be grafted the Moon waning, or not to be seen.'

The Seasons

Mr Williams used to say:

Drunk or sober,
Sow wheat in October

and

Who in January sows oats,
Gets gold and groats

He would always sow garlic and broad beans on the shortest day, advice I successfully followed in the days when I had a vegetable patch. Sow onions, he said, on St Gregory's Day (12 March) for a good crop. To do well, shallots should be sown on December 21st along with the garlic and pulled on the longest day (June 21st). Other pearls of wisdom included sowing potatoes when the yellow wagtail arrives in spring, usually March.

The Weather and Time of Day

Thomas Hyll, in his mid-sixteenth-century *The Sowing and Care of Seedlings,* tells us that 'seed must be sown on a mild, clear day and not when a north wind is blowing, nor the day verie cold, for in such seasons and dayes (as all the skilful report) the earth as then timorous and fast shut, hardly receyueth and nourisheth the seedes committed to it.'

Sometimes, however, country lore contradicts itself – hedging its bets perhaps: 'Sow dry and set in the wet', yet 'sow beans in the mud and they'll grow like a wood' and 'sow in a slop, 'twill be heavy at top.' 'If you can squeeze a handful of soil together and it sticks, it is too wet to plant.' And 'Sow barley when the sloe is white'.

Sow seeds in the afternoon when the earth is drawing in, and don't water newly set plants too late in the day – 'they don't like to be shivering in their shoes', as my gardener tells me.

Superstitions

Sowing seed can be a wasteful and expensive business when birds and other creatures think that we are providing for them: the son of a Lincolnshire gardener quoted his father's sayings:

Four seeds in a hole:
One for the rook, one for the crow,
One to rot and one to grow

and

One for the birds
One for the mice
Two for the master

Thomas Hyll, the sixteenth-century English gardener, suggests mixing seeds with soot before planting them: this protects them from birds and other predators and is surely worth a try to avoid disappointment.

For hundreds of years almanacs all over the world, such as Foulsham's *Old Moore's Almanack* in England, have given the best planting and sowing times for the garden.

Vox Stellarum:
Or, a Loyal
ALMANACK
FOR THE
Year of Human Redemption,
1753.
Being the Firſt after Bissextile or Leap-Year.
In which is contained all Things fitting for ſuch a Work; as,
A Table of Terms and their Returns; the Fulls, Changes, and Quarters of the Moon; the Riſing, Southing, and Setting of the Seven Stars, and other Fix'd Stars of Note; the Moon's Age, and A Tide Table fitted to the ſame; the Riſing and Setting of the Sun; the Riſing, Southing and Setting of the Moon; Mutual Aſpects, Monthly Obſervations, and many other Things uſeful and pleaſant.
Unto which are added,
Aſtrological Obſervations on the Four Quarters of the Year; an Hieroglyphick alluding to theſe preſent Times. A remarkable Chronology; the Eclipſes, and other Matters both curious and profitable.
By FRANCIS MOORE, Phyſician.
LONDON: Printed by J. Bettenham, for the Company of Stationers.

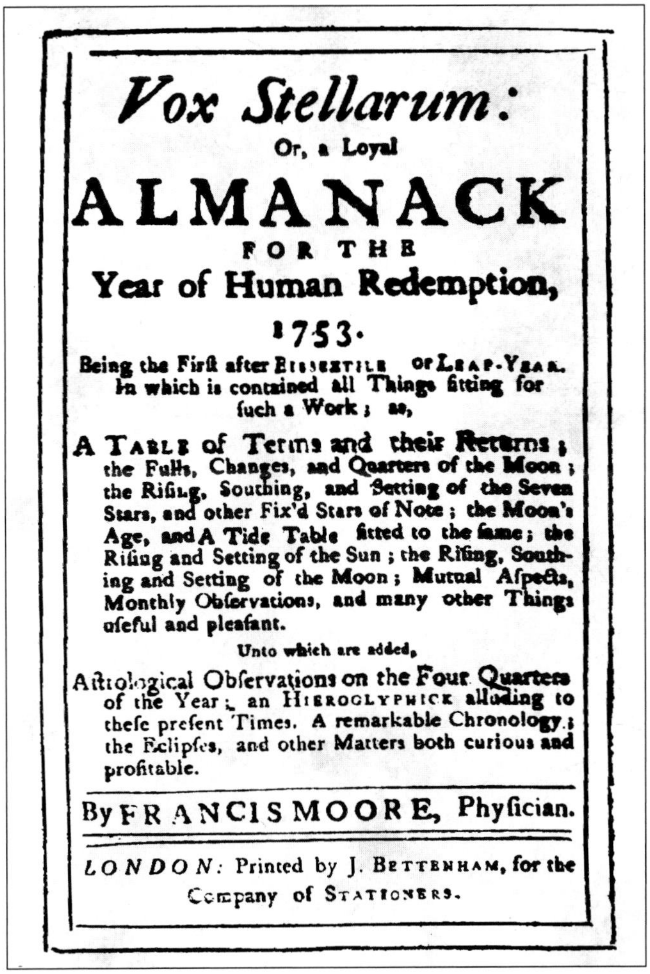

GARDEN PESTS

There are some plants that act as natural insecticides: chives and parsley deter greenfly, onion fly and carrot fly. Marigolds and nasturtiums repel whitefly, blackfly and greenfly, and wormwood repels everything. Tansy deters flies, ants and moths. Hyssop repels blackfly, pyrethrum controls aphids and spider mites, *Euphorbia lathyrus* repels moles, and onions among lettuces repel rabbits.

Planting 'plant decoys' is a smart move: whitefly loves nicotiana and aphids love basil, so use them as sacrificial plants near other, more precious ones. And encourage predators: create cover in your damp spots for toads and frogs because they eat pests, and encourage ladybirds by planting *Limnanthes*.

Slugs

Kate my editor remembers how her grandmother used to invert half-grapefruit shells with little 'doors' cut into them, to entice slugs in. In they came, whereupon grandmother would pick them up and crush them between her fingers. She still, according to Kate, uses this infallible technique. Kate's mother doesn't bother with the grapefruit but simply dispatches them between her fingers while carrying on a conversation! If you prefer a less tactile method, kill slugs by sprinkling them with salt. You can protect

Invert half-grapefruit shells with little 'doors' cut into them.

plants with a ring of sharp gravel around the bottom: this 'hurts their feet' according to the gardening expert Hugh Johnson. My gardener friend Barbara sprinkles crushed toasted eggshells around the plants – but above all she encourages her toads to do the work for her!

A friend in the village sinks a bowl of beer into the ground: the slugs fall in and drown (happy. . .). Slugs are repelled by a mulch of oak leaves or wood ash, and will also crawl under wooden boards where you can catch them unawares.

My mother's gardener used to strip the leaves from Brussels sprouts and lay them on the ground to distract slugs from the plants. He also laid prickly thistles, bracken or thorny evergreens near affected plants. He used to swear that if you put slices of turnip down for slugs they would die of overeating.

Ants

Ants are repelled by growing pennyroyal, spearmint or tansy. Such pests travel up tree trunks and you can stop them with a band of grease. Throw boiling water on the nest, says Barbara, or diluted Jeyes fluid. A medieval gardener suggests throwing sawdust from oak planks on to the ant hill. According to *Le Ménagier de Paris* (1393), the ants will then die or leave when it next rains, because the sawdust retains the water. But a Chinese friend whose father was a fruit farmer told me that, since ants eat the larvae of fruit flies, he used to make little bamboo bridges for the ants to travel from tree to tree!

Flies (aphids, blackfly, whitefly, and so on)

Ladybirds are one of nature's most efficient predators of fly. They particularly love *Artemesia* and *Limnanthes*, so if you grow some for them you will be well rewarded. Or you can simply spray with soapy water. Flies dislike spearmint, stinging nettles and nasturtiums, so these plants will act as deterrents.

An old Essex gardener told me of a natural – as opposed to chemical – way to get rid of the greenfly, blackfly and whitefly that plague the garden during the summer months: an infusion of rhubarb leaves, used as a spray. (This remedy is known in Australia too). It works. Put 900g (2lb) rhubarb leaves in a large pan with enough water to cover. Bring to the boil and simmer for 2 minutes. The leaves disintegrate quickly. Leave to cool, then strain. Store in bottles, in a cool place and use instead of chemical sprays. You can also make an effective spray by soaking nettles in rainwater for three weeks: this spray kills lice and aphids too (see page 69).

The same gardener told me to spray cabbages with sea water to deter caterpillars, but I have found a more whimsical remedy:

Go into the garden at dawn on Sunday and on bare knees say three Ave Marias and three Paternosters in reverence to the Trinity, then take a cabbage or some other leaf eaten by caterpillars and put inside two or three of them, and say 'Caterpillars come with me to Mass'; then take the whole thing along to church, and before listening to the Mass let it fall. After this the caterpillars will disappear from the garden — this is not a joke, it has been proved to work and its practice is still in use.

Girolamo Firenzuola, 16th century

Deer

There's not a lot you can do to keep deer out of a garden, apart from erecting a very tall fence all the way around. However, a Norwegian friend had this solution: go to the hairdresser and get a bag of human hair, fill small muslin bags with it and scatter them between your plants. Deer so dislike the smell of anything human that they will go elsewhere. The only trouble is that the hair must be fresh, and replaced frequently.

Mildew

My mother's gardener Mr Williams used horsetail tea to combat mildew. Take two large handfuls of horsetail, and put into a large pan with water to cover. Bring slowly to the boil and simmer very gently for 20 minutes with the lid on. Leave in a cool place for 24 hours and then strain. Dilute with two parts water and use as a spray. Liquid seaweed also gets rid of mildew, and chive tea is effective against mildew on gooseberry plants.

Birds, Spider Mites and Blight

If you scatter dried powdered garlic on the ground it stops birds eating nearby plants. Try this near your fruit bushes. Simplest of all,

Mildew on garden plants can be eliminated with horsetail tea.

get a predator on the job: have a cat patrol nearby, says Barbara. Garlic tea controls blight on potatoes and tomatoes, and spider mites you can easily deter with a spray of garlic or chilli pepper

Chilli Garlic Spray

3 hot green chillis
3 garlic cloves
3–4 teaspoons washing-up liquid
750ml (1¼ pints) water

Process the chillis and garlic finely in a small blender. Put into a bowl with the washing-up liquid and add the water. Leave to stand for 24 hours, then strain. Add a further 300ml (½ pint) of water to dilute, then pour into a bottle with a spray nozzle.

SOIL AND COMPOSTING

A gardener friend with a propensity to poetry tells me that adding chemicals to the soil makes it deaf to the music of the spheres. She is convinced that chemicals are toxic and the effects detrimental. She inherited a famous garden in Hertfordshire and has used totally organic methods to maintain – successfully – the stunning planting. Paths meander through great mature trees, and beautiful shrubs make a backdrop for herbaceous flowering plants in spring and summer. As you wander you come across a pond, a summer house, a spinney, and everywhere is designed for a vista. Her mother-in-law told her how to get rid of weeds on the many paved areas: sprinkle salt between the cracks. She also uses salt on the asparagus bed after it dies back, to keep the weeds down. Practical experience, hard work, and using much traditional country wisdom have contributed to the creation of a work of art.

Soil needs nourishment, which it gets from compost or humus – organic matter from decomposing plant and animal remains. So allow stinging nettles in your garden: they stimulate the formation of humus, the blackish-brown soil that you can see around a patch of nettles. You can also use seaweed extract as a soil conditioner.

Soil also needs trace elements to enable plants to absorb valuable minerals from the soil. Nitrogen is released into the soil by growing legumes, and clovers are the best fixers, along with blue lupin, alfalfa, peas, fenugreek and beans. Tobacco plants and tansy both accumulate potassium.

Leaf litter protects the topsoil and is an invaluable soil food, providing minerals and by-products which feed the microlife of the soil and indirectly the plants themselves. Microlife enhancement means enrichment: ancient wisdom says keep the ground covered with weeds in winter and the worms will turn the soil for you underneath. In addition, growing yarrow and valerian encourages worms and other creatures. Add some soot to the soil to enrich it and break it up. If your soil is very alkaline give it plenty of moisture and organic material.

Weeds are not necessarily always an evil: there are positive ways of looking at these much-maligned inhabitants of the garden, which have an advocate in the poet Ralph Waldo Emerson: 'What is a weed?' he declaims. Answer: 'A plant whose virtues have not

yet been discovered.' Some weeds are valuable mineral accumulators and thus can enrich the soil. By the law of return they feed the soil population which in its cycle builds up fertility: insect remains are of special value because the chitin which forms the body armour is believed to improve plants' disease resistance.

Other weeds aerate the soil and help with drainage: for example, dandelion and coltsfoot break up heavy clay. Some are

capable of lessening the impact of heavy rain on the ground. They provide shelter and food for small animals whose excreta help fertilize the soil. Hoeing weeds and leaving them to rot down helps to conserve moisture, as well as releasing nutrients into the soil as they decompose.

Liquid nettle manure poured on to the soil will promote plant growth and protect plants against unhealthy conditions. Cut the nettles, cover them with water and allow to decompose for three weeks. This liquid can also be used as a spray for foliar feed. Or soak a sack of horse manure in 15 litres (4 gallons) of water overnight, a Herefordshire gardener told me, and use to enrich the soil.

Compost

The art of composting is also a science, one which my friend Barbara, both plantswoman and gardener, has perfected. A stream runs through her beautiful garden, which is bordered by a cowslip

Nettles stimulate the formation of humus, and are an excellent companion plant for herbs. You can make a liquid manure from nettles.

Seaweed products release trace elements slowly back into the soil. They help resistance to disease and stimulate micro-life in the soil.

meadow. The vegetable garden, edged with a young yew hedge, is next to a formal rose garden full of old-fashioned roses. Her knowledge and understanding of how plants and soil work are the foundations of this exceptional garden. Set behind a wild flower area in one corner is a row of compost bins, all neatly cared for and surrounded by comfrey plants to layer in with the garden and household waste. Composting is an art form here: she dismisses the over-use of artificial fertilizers since they do not give the soil the structure it needs, and she feels that you can over-feed with chemicals and upset the balance of nature. If you work with rotted

compost, nature does it for you, and she just forks it in to the topsoil at the rate of one bucket per square metre. The Chinese use manure-based hot beds to warm the soil so that they can grow vegetables all year round, using both human and animal manure. They also make hot beds in greenhouses – using animal manure only.

Barbara separates herbaceous waste, weeds and household waste from grass clippings and leaves, which are kept to rot separately while tired topsoil, long grass and other bits and pieces are mixed with farmyard manure to provide phosphates, potash and nitrogen as well as humus.

Of her 14 compost bins, four are for household waste, four for grass clippings (in netting cages to allow air to circulate), two for leaves (best chopped by the mower, rather than left whole) and four for miscellaneous bits and pieces. They are turned regularly with a long-handled hay fork to let in air which activates the process of decomposition. There is nothing like compost, she declares, it is so rich in nutrients. Everything you take from the ground you have to put back. Everything natural can return to be recycled. She uses farmyard manure more for its structure than for the nutrients – roots need air and moisture so dig it in for an ideal growing medium. It makes a beautiful loam.

Compost Plants

Most annual weeds (except ones which have seeded) can go on to the compost heap – they contain valuable minerals which return to the soil and replenish it. Exceptions are perennial weeds such as couch grass, ground elder and bindweed which will only multiply in the compost. And don't put on any weed seeds as they will simply remain dormant until the compost is used. Some of the best compost plants include alfalfa, dandelion, bark of oak, camomile, valerian, comfrey, spinach, sunflowers, yarrow, and as many herbs as possible (except wormwood). Yarrow is a fast activator of compost.

Nettles (the leaves only, not the roots) make an excellent addition to the compost heap because they are so rich in minerals. They help fermentation and are an excellent soil conditioner. Barbara layers them in between other waste, including bonfire ash which provides iron, and she recommends lots of thin layers in the bin. You can use the friable humus around nettle patches as straight compost.

Comfrey is rich in potash, nitrogen and phosphates, so you can lay the wilted leaves on the soil as compost, particularly between rows of potatoes and around tomato plants in the greenhouse. Or put layers of comfrey between other compost: Barbara grows comfrey next to the bins so it is always handy. You can also make an excellent liquid manure from comfrey in the same way as nettles (see page 51).

Seaweed products release trace elements slowly back into the soil and make a gentle fertilizer. They help resistance to disease and stimulate microlife in the soil.

Don't put woody or thorny material on to the heap as it doesn't decompose – especially roses, which may harbour mildew or black spot. Conifers and other evergreens don't break down easily either. Don't put earthy roots on the compost heap: the earth will lower the temperature, and the roots of Brussels sprouts and greens may cause fungus problems. Potato tops may carry blight, so it is better to burn them.

Don't place your compost heap under conifers – their essential oils (used as a base for turpentine) retard fermentation. Never start compost on grass – remove the sods first since they also delay fermentation. Birch and elder trees seem to have a beneficial effect on compost bins placed nearby.

A gardener who opens her garden to the public told me that she digs in bits of old carpet and bolsters which rot away and enrich the soil. Even old boots will do, she tells me: the protein in the leather decomposes to produce nitrogen. Her annual herbaceous display of flowers and shrubs is heavenly. She gives her onions a top-dressing of soot during the growing season, and her magnificent lilies are nourished with wood ash. Her delphiniums, hollyhocks and sunflowers all benefit from fortnightly liquid lunches of beer, and her leeks love Guinness! Slightly milky water is also a good manure for herbaceous plants.

An Indian friend with green fingers mulches her roses with all the tea-leaves from the household, and sometimes crushed eggshells. Her mother swears by bananas: the skins are a rich source of magnesium, sulphur, silica and sodium, trace elements which ensure a magnificent show of flowers. She layers them just under the surface of the soil. I know several gardeners who water their roses with tea and claim that this increases their scent and encourages healthy growth.

It is no surprise, says Barbara, that allotments are proverbially so fertile: she observes that they have no public toilets, so a certain amount of 'recycled cider' returns to the soil. Slurry from sewage farms goes on to farmland, and rightly so. The idea of throwing it away into the sea or rivers is sacrilege to her. In her garden the walnut tree stands above their septic tank, and it is a huge healthy tree with lustrous leaves and abundant fruit. The grass in the meadow, above the weeper system from the house, is lush and verdant. 'The answer lies in the soil' indeed.

COMPANION PLANTING

Some of the great successes of gardening lore are to be found in the realm of companion planting. In Bulgaria, where vast quantities of roses are grown commercially for attar and rose oil, they are grown alongside onion and garlic crops. It has been shown that inter-cropping roses with garlic produces a far stronger perfume in the rose, an effect you can also get by fertilizing your rose bush with compost made from garlic and onion refuse. All the alliums have fungicidal properties and attract beneficial insects. Greenfly detest garlic.

Companion planting works in various ways. Some plants provide shelter from wind and sun, others give off root and leaf secretions which affect their neighbours either beneficially or adversely. Some plants may improve the soil by accumulating minerals, or by providing green manure or humus. Some may repel harmful insects and other pests, or act as decoys, or they may support insect populations which are beneficial to neighbouring plants. Or they may attract birds which prey on these pests. Some plants are found to reduce the amount of fungal and other diseases in nearby plants, due to their chemical secretions.

Growing sweet peas up sunflowers is a good example of symbiosis: the sweet peas release nitrogen into the soil while the sunflowers provide support and shelter. But there are examples of bad companions too: basil hates rue, tomatoes dislike fennel and kohlrabi, the brassicas and tomatoes don't grow well together. Garlic, onions and shallots inhibit the growth of beans and peas, and pumpkins dislike potatoes. Never grow raspberries with blackberries or radishes with hyssop. Tomatoes near potatoes have stunted growth, and the potato loses resistance to blight. Cabbages don't like the proximity of strawberries or early potatoes.

Herbs generally help plants growing around them, with the exception of fennel and wormwood which need to be grown in isolation.

Good Companions

Alliums are strongly scented and discourage pests from attacking nearby plants. Since they also accumulate sulphur, they have a fungicidal effect. They are particularly beneficial for carrots, tomatoes and lettuces.

Asparagus and tomatoes make excellent companions because root secretions from the asparagus kills *trichodorus*, a nematode that attacks tomato roots. In turn, the tomato guards against asparagus beetle. Parsley also protects against this beetle, so this trio thrive together.

Beans – especially broad beans – and potatoes grow well together, and potatoes repel the bean beetle. All leguminous species fix nitrogen in the soil which helps not only potatoes but also carrots, cauliflower, beets, cucumber and cabbage.

Cabbages thrive near aromatic herbs, whose leaf and root exudations deter pests. This is especially true of mint which repels the white cabbage butterfly. Tomatoes and celery help cabbages in a similar way, by deterring the cabbage white.

Cauliflowers grow well with peas, onions, potatoes and celery. Celery deters the cabbage-white butterfly, and celery and leeks grown together attract many beneficial insects especially predatory wasps.

Chives keep fungal diseases down, and next to carrots help them grow healthy and exceptionally tasty. They discourage black spot on roses, scab on apple, and guard against aphids on tomatoes.

Camomile grown next to peppermint makes both plants produce more essential oil. Camomile accumulates potassium and sulphur and is a host to hoverflies and wasps, so grown next to cabbage and onions improves them in both yield and flavour. Camomile's beneficial health-giving presence is well known to country folk who have nicknamed it the 'plant doctor', because planted near sick plants it helps them recover.

Aromatic herbs in general help plants grown around them, since their root and/or leaf exudations make them distasteful to pests.

You see few weeds around rosemary, rue and wormwood because these plants inhibit the germination of seeds. The secretions of wormwood are so strong that nothing thrives nearby, so it needs to be grown in isolation.

Foxgloves have a benign influence on most plants, stimulating their growth by accumulating potassium, iron and calcium, silica and manganese to high levels in their leaves which then drop and act as green manure to the soil around. They are especially good for pine trees.

Lettuces are good companions with chervil and dill since the herbs act as a decoy to aphids and other predatory insects.

Limnanthes douglasii, a famous bee plant, is excellent next to shrubs and soft fruit. It attracts pollinators as well as predators such as hoverflies. Insect remains and by-products add nutrients to the soil.

Mexican or African marigolds (*Tagetes* sp.) have a root secretion which kills minute parasitic worms known as nematodes. Grown near the greenhouse they keep whitefly off tomato plants since the odour of leaves and blossoms acts as an insect repellent. They also attract predatory hoverflies. They are excellent for keeping pests off roses.

Nasturtiums secrete root and leaf exudations which make them distasteful to pests. They help to keep whitefly from the greenhouse, aphids from broccoli and woolly aphids from the apple tree. Radishes thrive near nasturtiums.

Nettles (deadnettles, *Lamium* sp.) produce nectar for early bees and other insects, and are beneficial to vegetables. They may also deter the potato bug.

Onions repel carrot fly and carrots repel onion fly, so grown in alternate rows both thrive: the respective flies get confused! Onions go well with brassicas, tomatoes and lettuces since the strong smell keeps off pests. Next to strawberries they prevent mould on the fruit.

Peas, with their leguminous gift of fixing nitrogen in the soil, thrive next to radishes and all root crops, and radishes and chervil like each other. Nasturtiums nearby keeps pests away from radishes.

Runnerbeans and sweetcorn thrive together since the beans release nitrogen back into the soil which the corn uses, and the beans use the corn to climb up. Sweetcorn, peas and brassicas make a good trio, potatoes like the proximity of sweetcorn, and all squashes, including pumpkin, thrive with corn, an early discovery of the North American Indians.

Salsify helps leeks and carrots, repelling the carrot root fly.

Spinach and strawberries love each other. Spinach adds saponins to the soil which binds the humus together with coarser materials, helping it to retain moisture.

Yarrow helps all the aromatic herbs and is beneficial to all vegetables: a border of yarrow around the vegetable plot makes for a healthy harvest. It attracts worms and other creatures whose remains are of special value to soil life: chitin from their body armour is believed to help the plants' resistance to disease.

Bees, ladybirds and butterflies

Bees

There are five hundred bees for every human being on earth. We depend on them for crop pollination, so they are intrinsic to our survival on the planet. No wonder that bees have acquired such a special status in the eyes of country people who rear them, and who for centuries have found myriad uses for their honey and wax. They are welcome visitors to any garden, cross-pollinating as they collect nectar. One of the many staggering facts about bees is that it takes the nectar of one and a half million flowers to make a single jar of honey (see more about bees on page 146).

Beekeeping has been a part of rural economies worldwide for generations, and now thrives on a global commercial scale. Bees are held in awe for their industry and organization by all who work with them. Much garden lore has grown up around them as beekeepers watched them at work and established a relationship with the colonies in their hives.

A committed beekeeper in our village, a lady in her eighties, told me that catching a swarm of bees is only any good at the beginning of the season, and that later swarms will not settle in and produce good amounts of honey:

A swarm in May is worth a load of hay
A swarm in June is worth a silver spoon
A swarm in July is not worth a fly

'Telling the bees' is another widespread tradition, claimed by all who use it to have some mysterious truth to it: if you don't 'tell' them, you lose them.

Marriage, birth and buryin'
News across the seas,
All you're sad and merry in
You must tell the bees

If you don't, they fly away to seek the departed, or die themselves. Furthermore, all hives must be turned or moved at the moment their dead owner's corpse leaves the house for burial.

Ladybirds

There are five thousand species of ladybird throughout the world. In any garden they are nature's best method of controlling aphids, scale insects and mites. So efficient are these predators that when the Californian citrus industry was threatened with disaster in 1886 by an outbreak of cottony-cushion scale (*Icerya purchasi*), the Australian ladybug beetle (*Vedalia*) was imported to deal with it. Within a year the scales had all but disappeared. So always encourage them: they do a wonderful job on the fly in my garden, and I encourage them in my conservatory too.

Butterflies

Butterflies, beautiful as they are, are more of a mixed blessing. Although they are important pollinators as they visit flowers for nectar, the larvae or caterpillars will chomp their way through vast amounts of foliage, stems, flowers and even roots. There are over one hundred thousand species of *Lepidoptera* worldwide and they occur on every continent except Antarctica. The largest family groups are found globally, and agriculture, forestry, food, fabrics and fodder are all prone to the foraging of the various larvae. Yet quite possibly mankind also benefits from much unrecognized weed-eating by caterpillars, and it is incontestable that we benefit in the garden, as with bees, from flower pollination by the adult butterflies. A few butterflies feed on overripe fruit, so if you wish to attract the Camberwell beauty (rare) or the red admiral (found virtually the world over), leave your windfalls on the ground.

You seldom see butterflies flying in dull weather, and this is because they use solar energy to energize their wings for flight. Hence the common sight of a butterfly 'basking' in the sun before take-off.

Leave a corner full of nettles in the garden in which the Red Admiral can lay its eggs.

Plants for a Butterfly Garden

I talked to a butterfly gardener in his glasshouse, which was full of lantana, the prime butterfly plant which produces so much nectar. Butterflies taste with their feet, he informed me! Around us flowered plumbago, bougainvillea, and heliotrope, pentas, cestrum and jasmine. Hibiscus and morning glory intermingled, and a giant passion flower filled one corner of the glasshouse.

For the garden he advised leaving a corner full of nettles for the red admiral to lay its eggs. His wild garden included scabious, plantain, foxgloves, mallow, cornflower and some giant thistles. There was ragged robin in abundance and valerian scrambling along the walls. A patch of origanum attracted hordes of meadow browns, peacocks and small tortoiseshells. The commas loved the rotting fruit under the apple tree, and his lavender was covered with cabbage whites in high summer.

Honeysuckle

Among other herbaceous butterfly plants he recommended aubretia, buddleia, honesty, sedum, michaelmas daisy, sweet rocket, tobacco plant, yellow alyssum, golden rod, pinks, hyssop, lilac, honeysuckle, forget-me-not and violas.

Controlling Caterpillars

The most ecologically friendly way to control caterpillars is to hand-pick them off, rather than to use toxic sprays which may well do unseen damage to plants and friendly insects. At worst, use a plant-based insecticide such as the rhubarb spray on page 49. Some gardeners place a strip of foil around the root stem of cabbage seedlings to protect them from cabbage-fly larvae. Sprinkling crumbled mothballs over the soil around carrots and planting mothballs with potatoes does much to ward off both larvae of all kinds, and other pests.

SOME GARDEN FLOWER LORE

More in the garden grows
Than the gardener sows
Spanish Proverb

The earliest known medicines and antiseptics came from herbs and flowering plants, and so before their properties were understood scientifically they were believed to be magic. Much fascinating country lore accumulated over the ages, some based on their practical virtues, some imbued with superstition. Flower and tree lore is an enchanting combination of the two and in its immensity fills many volumes. Most famously, white wild flowers bring bad luck if they are brought into the house, and there are omens associated with flowers blooming out of season. The doctrine of signatures dictated many folk cures, and divination with plants was widely practised. Certain saints' days in the calendar have particular flowers associated with them, and rituals were enacted around the cultivation of many plants.

Here's flowers for you;
Hot lavender, mints, savory, marjoram;
The marigold, that goes to bed i' the sun;
And with him rises weeping.
William Shakespeare, *A Winter's Tale* (1610–11)

You can use the bright flowers of nasturtium to decorate a summer salad, and eat the peppery-tasting leaves.

Marigold Petal Salad

At the height of summer there are plenty of marigolds to spare for the table. Combine the petals with some nasturtium leaves and you have a deliciously unusual salad.

SERVES 2–3

1 oak leaf lettuce, washed and spun dry

1 handful nasturtium leaves, washed and shredded roughly

6–8 cherry tomatoes, halved

50g (2oz) toasted sunflower seeds

1 handful marigold petals

DRESSING:

2 tablespoons olive oil

2 tablespoons raspberry vinegar

1 tablespoon soy sauce

Combine all the salad ingredients, reserving a scattering of marigold petals for the top. Mix the dressing ingredients together and toss thoroughly. Garnish with the remaining petals, and it is ready to serve.

Marigold

The marigold opens as the sun rises and closes at sun-down: in Wales they say that if it does not open before seven, there will be thunder during the day. Some country people say that if you pick marigolds you will bring on a thunderstorm.

The marigold is a symbol of constancy in love. It was used in wedding bouquets and love potions and has local names of Summer's Bride and Husbandman's Dial. Used in love divination, marigolds were dried with summer herbs, powdered and made into an ointment with honey and vinegar. A young woman would annoint herself before going to bed, with an invocation to Saint Luke to dream of her true love.

Marigolds were believed to reduce fevers and even to repel the plague if you carried them about with you in the streets. The petals have long been used to tint hair golden-red, and a conserve was recommended by some herbalists to alleviate depression.

The marigold is a symbol of constancy and love.

Aconite is highly poisonous: arrows dipped in the juice were said to kill wolves, hence its alternative name of wolfsbane.

Broom has both sinister and beneficial qualities: a besom of blossoming broom would 'sweep the head of the house away', whereas the plant was a symbol of good luck and plenty and made its appearance at country weddings, tied with ribbons.

Box sprigs were often placed at the door of a house at which there was a funeral. Each of the mourners would pick one up and later drop it into the open grave. Box was often used in well-dressing.

Carnations have been cultivated for over two thousand years and their heavy scent was used in Elizabethan times to replace expensive cloves. To wear a carnation meant that the wearer was betrothed and other suitors might as well give up their pursuit.

Celandine was used as a cure for jaundice – by sympathetic magic because of its bright yellow colour. I have a friend in Suffolk who uses it on warts with success, and a grandmother in Oxford has done so for years. Just drop the fresh juice from the stem on to the wart and let it dry. Continue the treatment until it disappears.

Cherry: A good crop brings good fortune – 'a cherry year a merry year'. A friend of the family who lived in Switzerland for many years says that traditionally a new mother eats the first cherries to ensure a good crop for the rest of the season.

Cornflowers were reputed to blunt the blade of a reaper's sickle, and were once used as an ingredient of ink. Watercolourists still use the juice from the flowers, mixed with alum (see page 66). A courting man could divine his love life: he put a cornflower in his pocket and only if it lived would he marry his current girlfriend.

Daffodils: The Welsh say that whoever finds the first flower will have more gold than silver in the coming year. To point at a daffodil may stop it flowering.

Forget-me-not was useful against dog and snake bites! Steel tempered with its juice was said to be hard enough to cut stone. Give a forget-me-not to someone starting a journey on February 29th.

Lilac is unlucky in the house, especially white lilac (as with many white flowers). It is associated with death and it is unlucky to find a five-petalled lilac blossom.

Lily, symbol of virginity, purity and innocence, is a favourite flower at weddings and funerals. The madonna lily will only grow for a good woman, or where the mistress is master. A ninety-year-old woman who spent some years in the Belgian Congo in her youth and had some hair-raising experiences in the jungle, told me that the pygmies wore flame lilies in their belts to guard themselves against being eaten by a lion!

Marigold is a symbol of constancy in love, and a flower of the sun. A conserve or tea will allay depression, and a flower head rubbed on to a wasp or bee sting is an instant cure. Thunder may follow if you pick marigolds. Boiling the flowers produces a yellow dye, and the petals can be used in salad (see page 59). The volatile oil is a wound-healer.

Mulberry: When the leaves appear there will be no more frosts. It was a sacred tree in ancient Rome - and Burma! In China the mulberry is a symbol of industry.

Peach is a symbol of immortality throughout the Far East.

Pear is a slow-growing tree so, 'plant pears for your heirs'. It is considered a powerful charm against evil.

Periwinkle has long been thought to be a magical plant, and now the Madagascan periwinkle (*Vinca rosea*) is an important medicinal source of drugs used to treat leukaemia.

Plum 'A plum year is a dumb year' my grandfather used to say. A Welshwoman tells me that if a plum tree blooms in December it foretells a death. But to dream of plums is a good omen.

Quince is a symbol of love. To dream of quinces means you will be cured of any sickness.

Snowdrops are a symbol of hope and purity, yet in some places they are thought to be unlucky in the house. A single snowdrop is an omen of death.

Strawberries: A Norwegian friend tells the story of Frigga, goddess of married love, who is said to have hidden the souls of dead children in strawberries to smuggle them into paradise. Strawberries are dedicated to the Virgin Mary.

Violets: If they bloom early it means death or an epidemic, but to dream of violets brings good fortune. Worn around the neck they prevent drunkenness. I found a 'violet reviver' in a book of *Grandmothers' Recipes* of 1901, which claimed that boiling violet leaves in water and applying the liquid on lint as a compress was a cure for cancer (see page 119).

Yarrow is called *herbe aux charpentiers* because it was supposed to heal instantly wounds made by carpenters' tools. Achilles was said to have cured his warriors' wounds with its leaves, hence its botanical name *Achillea millefolium*. It has local names of 'woundwort' and 'nosebleed'.

Yew: Plant a tree at the south-west corner of the house for protection. Yew is the tree of immortality, being a long-lived evergreen which regenerates however hard you prune it. The reason that it is planted in churchyards is because all parts of the tree are poisonous: the volatile oil taxine can cause immediate death to children, cattle and sheep, and is therefore kept inaccessible to them. The alkaloid taxol is also an important constituent in an anti-cancer drug, and you can offer your yew clippings as raw material for its processing to firms who advertise collection from your garden.

Rub a marigold flower into a wasp or bee sting.

NATURAL
BEAUTY

Natural beauty care is grounded in centuries of tradition: the legendary beauty of Helen of Troy was not based on industrial synthetics. Cleopatra bathed in milk; Egyptian women perfumed their hair with marjoram, rubbed pomegranate juice into their skins and used rhubarb juice to counteract greasy hair and highlight the colour. Nature has always provided the human body with the oils, dyes, herbs, scents and emollients needed to repair and beautify it. By means of steams and face packs, compresses and sweet baths, oil treatments and hair washes, the body is beautified the natural way. Scientific analysis today is showing 'old wives' tales' to be true: the products work for reasons that we can now explain. The wisdom of our usually female ancestors is affirmed.

The advantage of making your own products is that you know exactly what has gone into them, and you can use pure substances which in the end are far cheaper than buying commercial products of similar quality. They are widely available throughout the world. Beeswax, cocoa butter, essential oils and good-quality base oils, mixed with infusions of fresh herbs, will give your body a new look and feel. And it is all quite simple to do, as my friend and aromatherapist Mary confirmed. Mary's grandmother was Scottish, and her mother lived in Australia for many years before returning to England.

Mary was an only child and her mother paid great attention to her long blonde hair. As a child she would squirm and rebel as she had her hair 'polished': her mother would take a pure silk scarf and stroke the newly-washed hair with it until it shone like spun gold. She told her daughter that your hair should 'squeak' when you run your fingers down it – meaning there was no residue of soap left after shampooing. This, she assures me, is the origin of 'squeaky clean'. And to get rid of split ends on this fair head of hair her mother used to twist or plait it, and singe the ends with a candle to take them off and seal the ends. It never caught fire.

Mary had a country childhood on a farm surrounded by woods and streams, with a full kitchen garden and huge barns full of chicken and geese. She learned about natural products from her mother in her childhood, and then travelled the world at a young age, through Turkey to Thailand, ending up for five years in the Bahamas. She picked up tips and customs as she went and has incorporated this knowledge into her professional practice. Her tips are practical and down to earth, yet infused with her love of the countryside and things natural. Her practical wisdom pervades all the recipes for natural beauty care: skin and hair, hands and teeth, eyes and body, and shows how we can look after our bodies in the natural way that women have used for centuries.

INGREDIENTS FOR HOME BEAUTY CARE

Many of the oils and other substances used in this chapter may not be familiar. Here is what they are, and where to find them.

Alum is a whitish transparent mineral salt which acts as an astringent. Available from chemists.

Ambergris is a greyish resin of waxy consistency secreted from the intestines of the sperm whale. It has been used in perfumery for centuries.

Borax is a salt (acid borate of sodium), used to remove grease and dirt. Available from chemists.

Benzoin, tincture of: Also known as 'the frankincense of Sumatra', this is a balsamic resin obtained from the styrax tree which grows in Indonesia and Vietnam. A tincture is a solution of the essential oil. Used as an antioxidant and fixative. Gum benjamin, as it is also known, crystallizes in shiny prisms and forms a brittle mass of whitish tears embedded in a translucent matrix. Available on order from chemists.

Almond oil is pressed from the seed of *Prunus amygdalus*, native of West Asia but extensively cultivated. Almond oil is a good emollient for all skin types and a useful base oil containing protein and many vitamins and minerals. Widely available from chemists and health stores.

Avocado oil is a heavy oil excellent for facial tissues and older skins. Its proteins, vitamins A and D and lecithin are easily absorbed into the skin. Widely available from health stores or chemists.

Beeswax in its pure form is available in blocks from some furniture and antique shops, and is very inexpensive for the quality ingredient that it is. It is an excellent moisturizer and enricher when used as a base for skin cream.

Castor oil comes from a shrub, *Ricinus communis*, native to India. Its prolific oval seeds are pressed for a viscid colourless oil which is an excellent skin emollient when mixed with other oils. Soothing for the skin and eyes.

Coconut oil is widely available, a rich oil pressed from the white meat of the coconut. It is often used to soothe sunburn.

Cocoa butter is a solidified oil (theobroma) used in many skin cream preparations. In its pure form it can be obtained from good chemists, but it is fairly expensive.

Essential oils are the concentrated oils of flowers, leaves, seeds, bark and roots of aromatic plants. They are very powerful and need to be used sparingly, usually in a carrier of base oil such as almond. The quality can be good, bad or indifferent, according to the country of origin, method of extraction and manufacture. They are sometimes synthesized, and often adulterated. To be sure of purity and quality, buy authentic oils from accredited aromatherapists.

Glycerine is a colourless syrup obtained from animal and vegetable oils and fats by saponification and is widely available from chemists.

Lanolin is oil washed from the wool of sheep after shearing. It acts as a protective lubricant and is an excellent softener and moisturizer. Use anhydrous lanolin which is not mixed with extra water. Available on order from chemists.

Orange-flower water is prepared from orange blossoms. Available from good chemists. You can make your own with dried blossoms (see page 94).

Pure alcohol is rectified spirits which are available on prescription only.

Rose-water is available from good chemists and apothecaries, or you can make your own version – undistilled – from scented rose petals. An important ingredient of many cosmetics.

Wheatgerm oil comes from the germ of the wheat grain and is highly nutritious, containing vitamins B and E – the latter being *the* skin vitamin. It is also antioxidant and helps stabilize essential oils and makes the preparation last longer. Widely available from health stores or on order from chemists.

Witch-hazel helps to preserve lotions and creams and is excellent for rough skin, spots and blemishes, or minor skin irritations. It is extracted from the leaves and bark of *Hamamelis virginiana* and is available from chemists. Mix with rose-water for an excellent skin tonic.

Natural Hair Care

Mary learned numerous tips from her mother, who cared for her hair as a child, and still applies this wisdom. She is emphatic about treating hair from the inside by eating raw fresh fruit and vegetables to provide essential nutrients. She advises drinking plenty of fresh water, and making sure that you are getting enough protein and B vitamins, especially those found in wheatgerm, soy, rice and legumes.

Mary's mother always extolled the virtues of the old-fashioned '100 strokes' where you put your head down and brush the hair forewards: this brings blood to the head, brings oils from the follicles into the hair and gives it a marvellous sheen. To improve it further, my Indian girlfriend, who has long glossy hair to die for, told me that if you cut your hair at the new moon it will grow thick as the moon waxes.

Hair Care

When she first left home and remembered that her mother had enriched her hair somehow with egg, Mary used whole egg by mistake, and the white began to cook in the hot water on her hair. It took for ever to rinse out: so remember, add egg yolk only to your shampoo! It is especially good for fine or limp hair.

For oily hair, use cider vinegar or lemon juice in the rinse water (150ml/¼ pint to 1.2 litres/2 pints): it removes all traces of soap and gives the hair lustre.

For dry hair, she suggests taking wheatgerm internally. Or warm 5 tablespoons of wheatgerm oil and pat on to the hair. Cover with a warm towel and leave for 30 minutes before shampooing. Be careful to protect your hair it from sun and sea winds, which dry it out even more.

You can make a great difference to the sheen and body of your hair by treating it with herbal infusions, tonics and rinses.

Herbal Hair Tonic

I tried this infusion in early summer when fresh herbs are at their best in the garden, and it gave my hair a fabulous sheen.

Make an infusion (see next recipe) of equal proportions of camomile flowers, rosemary, bay, sage and southernwood. When cool, massage regularly into the scalp when rinsing – it strengthens and feeds the roots of the hair, and stimulates the scalp tissues. Use more camomile for fair hair, more rosemary for dark.

Another time I added lime flowers, fennel, nettle, horsetail and yarrow, and the result was a thick lustrous head of hair.

Master Infusion Recipe

Rosemary stimulates the hair follicles, and regular use can prevent early thinning. I made this simple infusion for my partner to rub into his scalp to make his hair grow healthy and strong, and it has been a huge success. He uses it as a rinse every time he washes his hair, and it gives it body and lustre.

25g (1oz) dried rosemary, or a generous handful of fresh leaves
1 litre (1¾) pints water

Add the rosemary to the water in a pan. Bring to the boil and simmer for 10–12 minutes, covered. Leave to cool for 1–2 hours, then strain. It is best used at once, but can be stored in the fridge for a week, or until it starts to ferment.

Use this as a master recipe, and double the quantities of herb for a strong infusion. For dry hair use comfrey, elderflowers, quince blossom or sage. For oily hair, use mint, horsetail, lemon balm, lavender, marigold or yarrow.

Sage Infusion

This classic recipe stimulates the scalp and the hair, and consistent use darkens the hair. Make a strong infusion (see above). You can darken eyebrows by mixing it with several drops of olive oil and applying nightly using a clean mascara brush.

If you steep a slice of lemon peel in a small bottle of castor oil for several days, you have a mixture for longer, stronger lashes. At bedtime, brush the oil on your eyebrows and upper and lower lashes with a clean mascara brush.

Rosemary Oil

This is wonderful for my dry hair: infuse 25g (1oz) fresh rosemary in 600ml (1 pint) olive oil and leave it standing for a week on a sunny windowsill. Massage it into your scalp and wrap your hair up in a hot towel for 10 minutes before you wash it.

You can also make a nettle oil in the same way, for lustre and to stimulate growth.

Hot Oil Treatment

Mary's mother told her that to keep your hair in prime condition, gently heat 150 ml (¼ pint) virgin olive oil in a double boiler and apply to layered sections of the hair. Wrap your head in a warm towel and keep the oil on for several hours before shampooing. My Indian friend uses sesame oil, and during Mary's time in the Bahamas she recalls that the locals used coconut oil. A friend of hers from Bali uses manuka (tea tree) oil.

Nettle Tonic

A local country girl gave me this recipe that her grandmother had passed down to her. She had beautifully soft and glossy hair, and told me that this tonic, which she often used, improves and brightens the natural colour of hair. It also clears dandruff. Wear rubber gloves to gather the nettles!

225g (8oz) young nettle tops, washed
600ml (1 pint) water

Add the nettles to the water in a pan and heat slowly over a low flame. Simmer very gently for 3–4 minutes, keeping the lid on. Remove from the heat and allow to cool for 2 hours. Strain off just before use, and use as for the camomile rinse below.

Camomile Flower Rinse

This comes from a beautician who lived in South Africa for many years. It puts brilliant highlights into blonde hair.

100g (4oz) dried camomile flowers
750ml (1¼ pints) water

Follow the recipe for Rosemary Infusion, substituting camomile flowers for the rosemary. Warm gently to use. Rinse the hair several times, then leave on for 15–20 minutes before rinsing with cold water.

Beer Rinse

My cousin in the USA swears by this: allow a can of beer to go flat and use as an after-shampoo rinse (see Camomile Rinse, above). Stale beer is useful for setting hair because it gives it body.

Flat beer makes an excellent after-shampoo rinse.

HERBS FOR HAIR COLOUR

Fair hair: camomile, cowslips, great mullein flowers, nettles, turmeric.

Brown hair: cinnamon, cloves, henna, marjoram, parsley.

Red hair: ginger, henna, juniper berries, marigolds, sage.

Dark hair: elder leaves, henna, lavender, raspberry leaves, rosemary, sage, black walnut (*Juglans nigra*).

Pre-shampoo Conditioner

One of Mary's tips is to apply any conditioning treatment just before going into a sauna or steam-bath: the pores of the scalp open and take in maximum nourishment. Give yourself a treat!

Egg yolk is an excellent enricher of hair, keeping it beautifully soft. Some people have even told me that they use home-made mayonnaise: add 2 tablespoons cider vinegar to the rinsing water to help remove all the traces.

You can use safflower, almond or wheatgerm oil instead of the avocado used here. Coconut oil is an excellent pre-shampoo conditioner, especially in sunny countries where hair can suffer from becoming dried out.

> *2 egg yolks*   *A few drops of cider vinegar*
> *A few drops of glycerine*   *1 tablespoon avocado oil*

Mix all the ingredients together and massage into the dry scalp half an hour before shampooing. Rinse very thoroughly after shampooing, with a little lemon juice or vinegar in the water.

Castor Oil Conditioner

This strengthens hair and can be added to any combination of pre-shampoo conditioner. This mixture couldn't be easier to make.

> *2 tablespoons avocado oil (or oil of your choice)*
> *1 beaten egg yolk*
> *1 tablespoon castor oil*
> *1 tablespoon rosemary or sage (dark hair) or camomile (fair) infusion (see 68–9)*

Use as a pre-shampoo conditioner, as directed above.

Dandruff

My Indian friend's aunt had several Ayurvedic tips for dandruff: a paste made with young apple leaves used as a shampoo keeps it silky-soft, and also prevents premature greying and hair loss; and a paste of betel leaves and coconut oil prevents dandruff. Just washing your hair in cold water every morning without using a shampoo strengthens the roots of the hair and prevents dandruff.

Put 1 teaspoon cider vinegar into a glass of water and comb it through the hair morning and evening. Mary advises a lot of massaging of the scalp to stimulate the follicles – then the '100 strokes' to release oil into the hair. She gave me this recipe, which is used as a shampoo.

> *1 tablespoon chopped nettles*
> *150ml (¼ pint) boiling water*
> *1 egg white*
> *2 tablespoons mild liquid shampoo*

Make an infusion of the nettles and water. Beat the egg whites a little and add the shampoo. Strain the infusion into the mixture and use as a shampoo.

Mary recalled the silly days of the Sixties when straight hair was all the rage: she, along with her friends, would iron her hair under a damp cloth, contorting her neck to get her head on the ironing board. The lengths to which we will go for fashion …

TOP LEFT TO RIGHT: cinnamon, camomile, juniper berries, sage and turmeric can all be used to enhance hair colour the natural way. Make an infusion (see page 68), rub into the hair, leave for several minutes and then rinse out.

BALDNESS

Falling and thinning hair is often the result of stress, poor nutrition, prolonged illness or poor circulation. Seeing to these factors may help to remedy the hair loss. However, over the centuries many wild and wonderful cures have been claimed for baldness. Here are some of them:

Nettles have long been promoted as a cure for baldness. The Nettle Tonic on page 69 stimulates hair growth when rubbed well into the scalp every other night. Friends in New England sent me their family recipe:

1 part nettle leaves to 1 part onion to 100 parts alcohol (70°)

Soak the leaves and the chopped onion in the alcohol for several days. Strain off and massage the liquid into the scalp daily.

A French friend told me that rubbing watercress juice into the hair does the trick. She was also keen on 'treatment from within'. Make up a cocktail in a juicer:

⅓ lettuce juice (as many dark leaves as possible)
⅓ green pepper juice
⅓ carrot and alfalfa juice, mixed

Likewise rosemary, she said, delays thinning by boosting the rate of hair growth. Rub a strong infusion (see page 68) into the scalp on a daily basis.

Yarrow steeped in oil is an old English remedy for preventing hair loss and growing a luxuriant beard. A Moroccan woman recommends her mother's version: castor oil, walnut oil and alum (see page 66). A balding comedian tells me that rum rubbed into the scalp promotes its growth more than anything else he has known.

Mary was sceptical about cures for baldness but accepted the tonic effect of double strength infusions of sage, (see page 68) or a blend of any of the following:

artichoke leaves, lavender, lime blossom, maidenhair fern, marigold, nasturtium, nettle, quince blossom, rosemary, southernwood, thyme, vine leaves, watercress, willow leaves.

Use daily on the hair, and leave for 15 minutes before rinsing with cold water.

Some hints from Ayurvedic wisdom: massage into the scalp coconut oil mixed with lime juice; or fenugreek seeds macerated in coconut oil.

A wash to stop hair falling out, from Virginia, USA:

12g (¼ oz) fresh tobacco leaves
50g (2oz) rosemary leaves
50g (2oz) box leaves
1.2 litres (2 pints) water

Mix all together in a pan. Bring to the boil and simmer very gently for 20 minutes. Cool, strain and apply to the roots of the hair. before shampooing.

Among the more wacky ideas: an old gardener from Herefordshire told me his grandfather used to say that if you go to sleep wearing a cap of ivy leaves it would make your hair grow. 'Apply a poultice of chicken manure,' came from a French friend's grandmother. And from an eighteenth-century *Commonplace Book*:

To Remedy Baldness

This is a hard thing to cure, yet the following things are very good. Rub the head or bald places every morning very hard with a coarse cloth till it be red, anointing immediately after with Bears grease; when fifteen days are past, rub every morning and evening with a braised Onion till the bald places be red, then anoint with honey well mixed with mustard seed, applying over all a plaister of Labdanum mixed with mice dung and powder of bees; do this for 30 days.   William Salmon 17th century

If that won't stimulate the hair follicles, nothing will.

An eccentric country tradition has it that if you go to sleep wearing a cap of ivy leaves, your hair will grow back.

NATURAL SKIN CARE

Rafath's family live in Hyderabad and she and I travelled through India together some years ago. Her mother and grandmother had brought her up in a traditional Indian way as a close family, with many traditions and customs passed down through the generations. Rafath has a mass of thick black hair that falls down to her knees, and a smooth, ageless, nut-brown skin. It is impossible to tell her age. One of the youth-and-beauty tonics passed down through her family was drinking the juice of a fresh lime in a glass of buttermilk every morning. Her hands are beautifully cared for, her teeth pure white, and I was certain that she would have all kinds of unusual and inspiring tips for me. I was not mistaken.

Skin is an infallible indicator of general health: if the latter is good, your skin glows, it is clear and unblemished. If you are overtired, ill or stressed, your skin will be sure to show it. Commonplace wisdom is that treatment starts from within: give yourself lots of fresh fruit, vegetables and salads for essential vitamins and minerals, plenty of water to flush the system, regular exercise and the right amount of relaxation and sleep, and your skin will look and feel great. As Rafath comments, if you're not eating the right food, forget it.

She describes how Indian brides have a whole body massage prior to their marriage, with a paste of saffron or turmeric with thick cream and Bengal gram flour. They are then bathed in sandalwood essence after which their skin is silky soft and glowing. A simpler recipe from traditional Ayurvedic wisdom is to mix the juice of a fresh lime into a glass of whole milk and add a teaspoon of glycerine. Leave it to infuse for half an hour and then apply every night to the face, hands and feet. Let it dry and go to bed without washing it off.

Freshly pressed juices do marvels too. For a fresh-looking skin, boil a bunch of watercress in 600ml (1 pint) of water for 10 minutes, then strain. Add an equal amount of milk and a tablespoon of lime water, and drink every morning.

Indian brides have a whole body massage with saffron, cream and gram flour before their wedding.

Mary's Recipes

Mary has been making home-made creams for years, and waxes lyrical about the beauty of the pure ingredients that goes into them. But, she says, it is a bit like making bread: the creams never turn out the same twice, and different people's turn out quite differently even when they are using the same recipe. It is delicate work to prevent them separating as you stir – I used a small slim wooden spatula as I worked. Always label creams – if you put a jar of cream in the fridge someone might think it's mayonnaise...

Cleansing Cream

This master recipe works wonders for a dry and sensitive skin. Apply gently but thoroughly, and leave for a minute or two before removing with a toner such as a flower water (see Sweet Waters page 94).

60ml (2fl oz) rose-water
(see page 66)
18g (¼ oz) beeswax
30ml (1fl oz) wheatgerm oil
60ml (2fl oz) avocado oil
3–6 drops lemon verbena essential oil
A pinch of borax (optional)

Stand the rose-water in a bowl over hot water. Melt the beeswax in a bowl over gently simmering water. Add the oils, beating steadily with a small spatula. Trickle in the warm rose-water slowly, stirring until smooth. Remove from the heat and stir until the mixture cools. Then add the essential oil. Stir well, and add a tiny pinch of borax if it separates or is too thick.

Cucumber and Yarrow Night Cream

A beautiful shade of palest green, this deeply moisturizing cream leaves the skin soft and enriched. It is the best night cream I have ever used.

¼ cucumber, liquidized in a blender
30ml (1fl oz) double-strength infusion of yarrow (see page 68)

Strain the cucumber through muslin and squeeze to extract the juice. Mix with the yarrow infusion. Follow the master recipe above, using this instead of the rose-water, and essential oil of lavender or rose geranium in place of the lemon verbena.

Galen's Cold Cream

Mary gave me the precise quantities for this classic face cream, and it is the best I have ever used, softening and lightly fragrant. It has evidently stood the test of time. Galen, a Greek philosopher, lived in the 2nd century A.D.

30ml (1fl oz) rose-water (see page 66)
12g (½ oz) beeswax
60ml (2fl oz) almond oil
6 drops rose essential oil, or lavender

Heat the rose-water in a bowl by standing it over hot water. Melt the beeswax with the almond oil in a bowl over gently simmering water. Slowly trickle in the warmed rose-water, stirring well. Off the heat, add the essential oil and stir until cool. Place in a pot with a lid.

Yogurt

Yogurt, like buttermilk, contains lactic acid and helps oily skin because of its acidity. My Indian friend often adds 1 tablespoon yogurt to a facial treatment, or uses it as a splash. Yogurt bleaches the skin slightly so it is useful for reddened skin or to bleach freckles.

Soured cream is good for dry skin. The lactic acid attacks bacteria and dirt and keeps the skin elastic and young-looking. Use on its own as a face splash, or add to other facial treatments.

Oily Skins

Lemon is an excellent cleanser, restoring natural acidity to the skin. It bleaches freckles and helps oily skin, used with beaten egg white. Add to rose-water (page 66), brandy or white wine as a blackhead and acne treatment.

Dry Skins

Dry skins need regular moisturizing, and benefit from herbal and flower waters (see page 66). A few drops of cider vinegar are beneficial added to every skin treatment. Vinegar tones the skin, cures flakiness and counteracts excess dryness with its restorative acidity. Add water to cider vinegar in a ratio of 8 parts water to 1 part vinegar, and finish with a few drops of rose oil.

SCRUBS

Cornmeal can be used as a scrub to remove rough skin and dead cells. Mixed with milk it will remove dirt and grime from the skin. Rafath's mother told me that soogi, the Indian cornmeal, is excellent because it is fine and not too abrasive.

Honey and Oatmeal Scrub

Oatmeal can be used in the same way, raw or cooked. You can use porridge oats, or mill them in the blender to refine them a little. Oatmeal is nourishing, it dislodges dirt, draws out impurities and heals rough skin. Try this:

1 egg yolk

2 tablespoons medium oatmeal

1 tablespoon olive oil

1 tablespoon runny honey

5 drops cider vinegar

Mix all the ingredients together. Apply to a clean face and leave for 20–30 minutes. Rinse off with warm water and finish with a flower water (see page 94)

Camomile Oatmeal Scrub

A classic from Mary's collection.

2 tablespoons strong camomile infusion (see page 68)

3–4 tablespoons fine oatmeal (process porridge oats in a small blender)

3 tablespoons warm milk

Mix to a paste of a holding consistency. Leave to soak for 2–3 minutes then gently rub on to the face, avoiding the eyes. Leave for 10 minutes, then rinse off with warm water.

Blemishes

A very simple old country recipe for a facial wash to remove skin blemishes is to peel an onion and put it into a glass of water. Cover with cling film and leave to soak in the fridge for 1 hour before use.

You can dry up blemishes with white wine, cider vinegar or lemon juice. Or rub watercress into the skin to remove a rash. In Bahamian bush medicine skin problems are dealt with by slicing aloe vera, rubbing it into the affected area and then sticking the plant to the skin. Healing takes place within twenty-four hours.

Bread Poultice

Mary swears by a bread poultice which she has used ever since her childhood. Wrap a slice of bread in muslin, dip into very hot water and apply as hot as possible to the skin. Leave on until cool. Her mother used to used a poultice of cooked carrots in the same way.

Calendula Oil

This can be used on scarred or damaged skin and is useful for treating nappy-rash, bedsores and bruises.

50g (2oz) marigold petals, crushed with a pestle and mortar

250ml (8fl oz) virgin olive oil

Put the petals into a glass screw-top jar and add the oil. Cover and leave on a sunny windowsill or in the greenhouse for 4–5 weeks. After 2 weeks, strain the oil through muslin, pressing out every drop. Add fresh petals and repeat the process. Shake the jar thoroughly daily. Finally strain through muslin into clean bottles and seal.

From Rafath's aunt who is an expert in Ayurvedic applications: rub fresh lime peel over pimples and it cures them permanently.

A bread poultice draws out spots and even splinters.

Skin Care for Men

Herbal Aftershave

This is a superb astringent with a woody, slightly spicy fragrance. My partner now uses it all the time in preference to any other. It soothes the skin and heals blemishes.

4 teaspoons tincture of benzoin or vodka

12 drops essential oil of bay leaves or benzoin

3–4 drops each essential oil of rosemary and rose geranium

60ml (2fl oz) rose-water (see page 66)

125ml (4fl oz) witch-hazel

Pour the benzoin or vodka, which act as a preservative, into a large bottle and add the essential oils. Shake well. Add the rose-water and witch-hazel.

Aftershave for Oily Skin or Acne

I gave this to a young man who had suffered acne for years, and he reported that it worked wonders.

2 drops each of lavender, geranium and bergamot essential oils

5 teaspoons vodka

200ml (7fl oz) orange-flower water (page 94)

100ml (3 ½fl oz) witch-hazel

Add the oils to the vodka and shake well. Add the orange-flower water and witch-hazel and shake again.

From my gardener: If you cut yourself while shaving, try rubbing on a handful of fresh yarrow leaves to stem the flow of blood. Or use witch-hazel, which doesn't sting nearly so badly as alcohol-based aftershaves from over the counter.

COMPLEXION

Gathering dew on May Day morning is a long-established country tradition for those who wish to have a fair complexion: young girls would rise early and bathe their faces and necks in the pristine dew from grass, aromatic herbs, lady's mantle (*Alchemilla mollis*) or may blossom (hawthorn – *Crataegus* sp.) for a beautiful skin. A distillation of tansy was also renowned for promoting a clear complexion.

A cottage remedy from the north of England suggests broad bean pods soaked in wine and vinegar, then mixed with very fine cornmeal and milk to make the complexion smooth and soft. Country folk say that if you eat watercress regularly it will give you a clear complexion. Likewise dandelion leaves have the same effect.

European ladies in the seventeenth century used lemon on their skin to give them a fashionably pale appearance, and lemons have always been used to improve the delicate colour of the skin. So if your colour is redder than you would like, rub a cut lemon over your face.

Mary told me that if you have broken veins and capillaries on your face, rub on camomile herbal oil (camomile flowers macerated in oil) and dab on regularly until they diminish.

Buttercup Lotion

A woman in the village who has lived in the country all her life gave me this delightful recipe. She tells me that you can substitute elderflowers and add a few drops of lavender water, and both these will ensure a radiant complexion.

225g (8oz) petroleum jelly
4 large handfuls of buttercup flowers (not the stems)

Melt the petroleum jelly over a gentle heat in a pan. Put in the buttercup flowers so that the jelly just covers them, and simmer very gently for 45 minutes. Strain, and place in a pot with a lid. Rafath's aunt has this recipe from Ayurvedic texts: spread grated apple over your face and leave for an hour for a beautiful complexion and to banish any blemishes in the skin.

The Moroccan maid of a French friend gave me her mother's recipe for improving the complexion: make a paste with yeast, flour and almonds and cover the face with it at bedtime. Wash off in the morning with rose-water. Or, she said, make a paste of egg yolk, muddy clay, cloves, benzoin and coriander with orange juice to mix. Apply as a face mask and leave on for 24 hours. A simpler idea was to macerate cloves in olive oil and use as a lotion on your face every evening.

Lady's Mantle Lotion

A stunning complexion cream that I have made many times. It is softening and non-greasy: the best.

25g (1oz) lanolin, available from chemists
90ml (3fl oz) almond oil
4 teaspoons wheatgerm oil
3–6 drops violet or geranium essential oil
25g (1oz) lady's mantle infused in 600ml (1 pint) water for 30 minutes.

Measure 30ml (1fl oz) of the infusion, then follow the master recipe on page 68.

This advice from a *Handy Hints* book of the late nineteenth century echoed a lotion that the Moroccan girl Rajina told me about, into which she had mixed ground up egg shell.

To Render the Complexion Fair

Bruise some sweet almonds in a mortar, and add water very gradually, a pint to 20 or 30 almonds; add sugar to prevent the separation of the oil from the water. Mix immediately, strain through a flannel, and perfume the mixture with orange-flower water.

Complexion Herbs

Certain herbs have specific effects, so you can make infusions of these herbs (see page 68) to add to the master cream on page 75 to suit your skin.

Lime flowers: improves circulation, smooths wrinkles, slightly bleaching.

Camomile: soothing, astringent, healing.

Peppermint: stimulates circulation and is disinfectant.

Fennel: smooths wrinkles, good for the eyes.

Rosemary: warming, improves blood supply, stimulating. Good for skin and hair. Used for centuries.

Elderflowers: cures sunburn, removes freckles and wrinkles, softens and cleanses the skin. Used since ancient times.

Lime flowers: to cleanse and refine.

Yarrow: for oily skins, and good for chapped hands.

Nettles: improves both skin and hair.

Marigold petals: healing for acne, scar tissue and rough skin.

Sage: cooling and astringent, good for skin and hair.

Lady's mantle: Used by the Arabs in cosmetics. Astringent and restorative for the skin. Helps inflammation and acne and can be used to lighten freckles.

Washing in the May Day dew is said to give you a beautiful complexion.

Left to right: almond oil, olive oil, Rosemary Astringent Lotion, peanut oil, Lettuce Milk Lotion and lanolin (front).

LOTIONS AND OILS

There is no need to rely on industrial synthetics; nature supplies us with numerous oils and lotions.

Hot Oil Treatments

You will get to know which oils suit your skin type. Mary, with her fair skin, swears by almond; Rafath, with her Indian skin, uses sesame and also recommends peanut oil highly. Olive oil works wonders on my dry skin. Whichever you use, hot oil treatments are a treat.

Olive Oil is excellent to soften the skin. Simply warm the oil and apply with cotton wood pads. Allow to soak into the skin for anything up to 30 minutes, then wash off with warm water and finish with a flower water (see page 94). The very first face creams of two thousand years ago were based on olive oil.

Peanut Oil (ground-nut oil) is particularly good for the dry skin on the neck. Draw your hair up from the hairline and heat up 5 tablespoons of peanut oil. Dip a large piece of cotton wool into the oil, squeeze out the excess and wrap around the neck. Lie down on a towel and leave until cool, then apply a second wrap.

Almond Oil has been used since the days of the ancient Greeks to restore the skin's natural oils which dry up under the Mediterranean sun. It keeps the skin lubricated and makes an excellent base for creams and lotions for all skin types, being rich in vitamins and minerals.

Buttermilk on its own is an excellent facial skin conditioner, used as a simple face splash. *The Art of Simpling* of 1656 suggests soaking tansy in buttermilk for nine days, then using it as a face lotion. Apply with cotton wool pads.

Coconut Oil is a tropical oil with a scrumptious scent which does wonders for ageing skin as well as giving shine to hair. A wonderful oil for after-sun care.

Lanolin (see page 66) is a sensitive copy of your own skin oil and can be mixed into oils and lotions for extra effect.

Honey and Almond Softener

Honey acts as a moisturizer and softener, and heals blemishes. This lotion is wonderful for daily face care.

50g (2oz) lanolin   *25g (1oz) almond oil*
25g (1oz) honey

Melt the lanolin in a bowl over simmering water. Add the honey and whip with a wooden spatula. Slowly beat in the almond oil. Remove from the heat, stir until cool, then bottle.

Lemon Lotion for Oily Skins

This makes the skin pearly and clear. It is cleansing and purifying and restores natural acidity to the skin.

1 egg white   *Juice of half a lemon*

Whip the egg white to a froth and add the strained lemon juice. Heat gently over hot water until the mixture thickens. Bottle and label. Store in the fridge for up to a week.

Hand Lotion

This is surprisingly effective for something so simple. The recipe comes from Mary's Scottish grandmother. Glycerine is a natural moisturizer that helps tissues to retain water, and is a good softener. It can be obtained from chemists.

Juice of 1 lemon
90ml (3fl oz) rose-water
60ml (2fl oz) glycerine

Mix the three ingredients together. Rub evenly into dry or chapped hands.

Lettuce Milk Lotion

Lettuce has been used in beauty treatments for centuries. Mary introduced me to this lotion which is sensationally good as a conditioner for all skin types.

1 head of lettuce
Water to just cover

Place the lettuce and water in a pan and bring to the boil. Simmer slowly for about 45 minutes. Cool a little, then strain. Add a few drops of tincture of benzoin as a preservative. Store in a labelled jar.

Rosemary Astringent Lotion

A refresher for all skin types.

7 tablespoons rosemary water   *5 tablespoons orange-flower water*
  (see page 68)   *1 tablespoon witch-hazel*
½ teaspoon borax

Mix the rosemary water with the borax in a bowl and stir until the borax has dissolved. Add the orange-flower water and witch-hazel and pour into a screw-top bottle.

Lady's Mantle Lotion for Spotty Skin

An elderly lady gave this recipe to Mary, who has made it up frequently for her clients. It opens the pores, clears excess oiliness and does wonders for spotty skins.

2 tablespoonfuls of lady's mantle leaves   *75ml (2½fl oz) buttermilk*
75ml (2½fl oz) boiling water

Make an infusion of the leaves and water (see page 78). Cool, then strain. Add the infusion to the buttermilk and use as a lotion.

EYES

According to country wisdom, garden dew is good for the sight, as well as giving a fair complexion. Thinly sliced cucumber reduces puffiness and eye strain. The Egyptians call lapis lazuli 'Stone of Heaven', and believe that it improves the eyesight along with emerald and quartz. A traveller friend who had just returned from Australia told me that an Aboriginal cure for blindness or poor sight was to place a grain of sugar in each eye.

Mary considers the herb eyebright, available in decoction or tincture form from herbalists, the best of all for eyes. The French call eyebright *casse-lunette* – because you can throw away your spectacles after using it! To the Germans is it 'consolation to the eyes', to the Italians *luminella*.

Cornflower Compress for Tired or Weak Eyes

A French friend tells me that the women in her village use cornflower for gritty eyes or irritated skin around the eyes:

Add 1 heaped teaspoon dried cornflowers (or 1 tablespoon fresh) to 300ml (½ pint) boiling water. Steep for 5 minutes, then strain. Soak several layers of lint, cut into rounds, in the lukewarm infusion and place over each eyelid. Lie down and relax for 5–10 minutes.

You can make an infusion of dried cornflowers to soothe irritated eyes.

A cold tea poultice is good for sore or tired eyes – especially Earl Grey, because the bergamot in it is uplifting and soothing. For weak eyes bathe them in cold water with a few drops of cider vinegar added. A witch-hazel compress is effective too: first apply a thin layer of wheatgerm oil to reduce the stinging effect. Rue flowers steeped in white wine were said to sharpen the eyesight.

Some Gems of Ayurvedic Wisdom

(via Rafath's aunt)

• Eat a cardomom seed daily with a tablespoon of honey to improve the eyesight.

• Use fresh onion juice with honey for eye disorders.

• Use drops of fresh pomegranate juice for eye strain or conjunctivitis.

• Placing the pulp of a baked apple over your eyes for 1 hour before retiring to bed cures eye strain.

For a Stye

Rub it with a gold wedding ring or with the hair of a black cat's tail.

The Arabs of North Africa use the juice of cotton-lavender (*Santolina*), sometimes mixed with milk, to soothe and protect the eyes from the wind and grit of the desert.

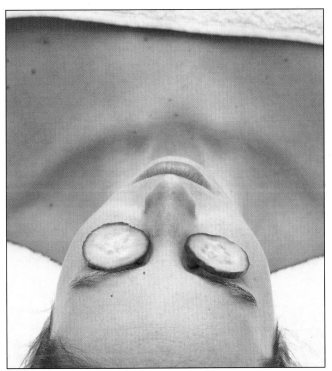

Cucumber has a cooling and restorative effect on the eyes.

TEETH

'A diamond is not as precious as a tooth', writes Cervantes in *Don Quixote*. Teeth which fall out during the seventh year of age should be preserved: in later years they have the power of relieving toothache. 'Hen's teeth' is an expletive to express the same sentiment as 'pigs might fly', and a correspondent from Michigan sent me this proverb:

> *If your teeth lie one on the other*
> *You will always live with your mother*

On a visit to North Africa our Moroccan maid Rajina told me that her grandmother used to brush her teeth with a mixture of charcoal and rock salt. In Britain a charcoal tooth powder used to be on sale and people also used to rub their teeth with the ashes of burnt bread, or burnt ground hazelnuts – said to be the best of all. This all tied in with my Indian friend Rafath telling me to use charcoal to clean my teeth – the rough bits that get in between the teeth act as floss. She told me that in India they chew betel

leaves to protect the teeth from decay and to freshen the breath. Mary told me that when she was in Thailand they would chew betel nut, and the fibres had a brushing action. Burnt aubergine is another of her tips. For sweet breath, chew mint leaves, or a cinnamon stick.

You can also clean teeth effectively with salt: moisten the salt and rub on with a soft brush – it is good for the gums, too. Ayurvedic wisdom suggests adding some pepper. My mother used to use bicarbonate of soda. To whiten teeth, rub with sage leaves, my old gardener told me. Or chew lemon rind instead of using toothpaste. Chewing a slice of lemon is good for toothache.

Strawberries are good tooth cleaners – just squash a strawberry through the mouth to leave it feeling fresh and to prevent tooth discoloration. Leave on the teeth for 5 minutes, then rinse off with a weak solution of bicarbonate of soda.

Cures for Toothache

Suffolk: carry a hazelnut with two kernels, chew yarrow leaves.
Cambridge: chew an elder twig.
Herefordshire: carry a gall from a wild rose in your pocket.
Traditional: rub with oil of cloves, or with onion juice; rest your face on a pillow of warm hops.
Russia: chew fresh ginger, or bite on a cube of sugar soaked with essence of leaf buds of birch – a sure cure.
Austria: wash the mouth with a blackberry leaf infusion.
India: rub with a pinch of powdered pepper mixed with clove oil, or chew mango leaves.

My mother used to use bicarbonate of soda to clean her teeth.

FRECKLES

In the past, Victorian ladies seeking the fashionably pale look used three parts fresh lemon juice to one part rum to treat their freckles. Although freckles are no longer considered unsightly, my daughter, who complains of too many, has been the guinea pig for these potions, and they work!

Anti-freckle Lotion

A simple remedy, easy to make and highly effective.

> *30ml (1fl oz) lemon juice*
> *¼ teaspoon powdered borax*
> *1½ teaspoons rosemary oil (see page 00)*
> *30ml (1fl oz) tincture of benzoin*

Rub a cut strawberry on to freckles to make them fade.

Mix all the ingredients together and leave to stand for a few days before using. Rubbed on the hands and face it will lighten the skin and eventually make the freckles disappear. Apply where required morning and night, gently dabbing the affected area with cotton wool or a soft cloth.

Buttermilk

This is a mild bleach and an effective treatment for freckles: Marie Antoinette used a compress of buttermilk to remove hers. Here is a country recipe given to me from Germany. If you have a very oily skin you can use yogurt instead of buttermilk.

> *6 tablespoons buttermilk*   *1 teaspoon grated horseradish*

Mix the milk and horseradish together. Lightly oil the face with olive or almond oil. Apply the mixture to unwanted freckles and allow to dry for 20 minutes. Wash off with tepid water. Rinse, and oil the face lightly.

Culpeper recommends rubbing bruised watercress leaves into freckles to remove them. A late nineteenth-century book of household hints suggests mixing the juice of a lemon with 1 tablespoon powdered borax and 1 tablespoon icing sugar. You apply it to the freckles, leave on for 20 minutes, then wash off with warm water. Cream the face after rinsing.

Strawberries can be used cosmetically to improve the complexion and lighten freckles. Use them in any facial (see page 90), or just rub the cut surface of a strawberry on to the skin. They bleach it mildly, making freckles less apparent.

The adverse effects of over-exposure to the sun are well known and most people are aware of the dangers of developing skin cancer. Until quite recently it was distinctly unfashionable to acquire a tan: it was regarded as coarse and a sign of the labouring classes.

Too much sun dries the skin and the natural oils need to be replaced. Burns need to be soothed. Certain oils and flowers – including lavender and elderflower – are highly effective in these treatments, and the ones you make are a good deal cheaper than the ones you can buy.

Elderflowers

Elderflowers are renowned as a skin herb. A friend in the next village gave me this excellent and effective lotion to refresh the skin after sunburn, which also counteracts the drying effects of swimming in salt water. It is best kept in the fridge and applied cold.

Several handfuls of elderflowers
Boiling water
50ml (2fl oz) pure alcohol (available on prescription)

Press the elderflowers into a large jar and fill it up with boiling water. Add the alcohol, cover with a tea towel and leave to stand in a warm place for 2 hours. Cool, strain and bottle, and cork well. Rub into the skin where required, or put some into the bath.

Elderflower Water

You should apply this when the moon is waning!

Pack as many elderflowers into a large jug as will fit, and pour over them at least 2.2 litres (4 pints) boiling water. Cover with a cloth so that none of the steam can escape. Leave to stand for 24 hours, then strain and bottle.

Honeysuckle Ointment

Mary's long-term standby for burnt skin is this lovely scented ointment that can bring soothing relief to sunburn and other minor burns. Lavender works really well too, in place of the honeysuckle, and marigold petals extend the healing properties of this remedy.

75g (3oz) petroleum jelly, available from chemists
3 heaped tablespoons honeysuckle flowers

Bring the petroleum jelly to the boil with the flowers and simmer for 20 minutes, stirring from time to time. Strain into warm jars and leave to cool before covering and labelling.

Sunburn

As we all know, it is not good to expose our skin to too much sun, but if we do over do it, it is wise to find mild relief in some of the following cures.

Sunburn Cures

From an American friend of my daughter: rub two strawberries over your face and leave the juice on for about half an hour. Wash off with tepid water, with a few drops of tincture of benzoin added to the rinse.

She also suggested making a face pack of crushed wild strawberries for a bad case of sunburn.

A Greek once told me that a good way to relieve sunburn is to wash the face with sage tea. Strong tea, cooled and applied on a soft cloth, soothes sunburn, and so does live plain yoghurt. Cider vinegar stings but relieves the burning.

HANDS

Softening lotions for 'household hands' can be made from a range of everyday products including potatoes, lemons and bananas. Rafath my Indian friend told me that if you cut up an aubergine and soak it in water, then use the water on your hands and face, it has a refining effect on the skin. Tamarind pulp has the same effect. Her grandmother's recipe was even simpler.

Grandmother's Lotion

5 parts glycerine to 15 parts rose-water

Simply rub into roughened hands. You can add a pinch of borax if the hands are stained.

This variation is fragrant:

60ml (2fl oz) glycerine   *Squeeze of lemon*
12 drops lavender oil   *90ml (3fl oz) elderflower water*

Mix together and rub into the hands.

Glycerine and rose-water make a simple hand lotion.

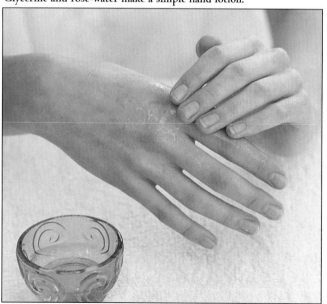

Lemons

• Rub lemon halves over roughened elbows to soften them.
• Whiten reddened housework hands with lemon juice.
• Massage a mixture of lemon juice and honey into rough, dry hands to make them soft and white.
• Rub lemon into nails to make them really clean.
• Use cider vinegar and water (1:8 parts) for softening the hands.
• From Mary: the essential oil of benzoin added to a base cream with lemon juice is wonderful for cracked hands (and feet).

An Indonesian friend declares that this makes a wonderful hand cream: mix 1 tablespoon mashed banana with 1 tablespoon sunflower margarine. She also told me to mix coconut milk and glycerine and rub it into hands and feet to soften them: this I have found to be incredibly softening.

Nails

Soft or brittle nails can be a real problem. Several country friends have told me that parsnips are an excellent internal help for brittle nails – eat as many as you can. If you have a juicer, juice them and drink it regularly, or make soup. Likewise, drinking cucumber juice helps to prevent splitting nails and also falling hair.

Mary advises eating masses of parsley, and soaking the nails in almond oil regularly – 10 minutes daily for several weeks if they are bad. Rub cocoa butter into the cuticles. I treat myself to a manicure where my hands are covered in hot paraffin wax and left to soak under clingfilm. Beeswax does a wonderful job too.

Horsetail and mugwort are both herbs that improve nail condition. Make a double strength infusion (see page 68) and soak the nails in it for 10 minutes daily.

An Indian superstition: never cut your nails after sunset, and never let the parings fall on to the floor, let alone step on them, for that will bring bad luck.

The water left after soaking a chopped aubergine has a refining effect on the skin, according to Ayurvedic wisdom.

WRINKLES

A French woman with beautiful skin told me that she always sprays her face lightly with a mineral water atomizer before putting on her make-up, and that this moisturizing process helps prevent wrinkles. In general, keep the face well lubricated with oil since dry skin wrinkles more easily: anhydrous lanolin, coconut or almond oil are all good. They are even more effective mixed with egg yolk or honey. Homemade mayonnaise is a good anti-wrinkle device too.

A young woman from New Zealand with a good sense of humour told me that the Maori answer to wrinkles was to get tattooed – and this was their answer for balding as well. My Indian friend Rafath has always used mustard oil to soften her face and she has no wrinkles! Rajina the Moroccan girl gave me her grandmother's recipe *pour ne pas vieillir*. Mix honey, ginger, cloves and nutmeg. Take 2 spoonfuls midday and evening. Another tip was adding ground melon seeds to egg yolk and applying it to the face at night, then washing it off in the morning with one of the world's most wonderful rose-waters, from the Dades valley in the Atlas Mountains.

My tip for a quick fix for wrinkles: pierce a vitamin E capsule and mix the contents with a little lanolin. Dab on and allow to soak in. Wipe off with a flower water (see page 94). Simpler still is to use pure wheatgerm oil, which contains vitamin E, a prime skin conditioner. Dab it on the face with cotton wool pads, leave to soak in for an hour, then clean off with rose-water.

Coconut oil used in the same way prevents dryness around the eyes and prevents heavy wrinkles. Rafath swears by it and recommended me to sleep with a mask of warm oil on the face (see page 80). She also described how a pulp of ripe banana mixed with a teaspoon of rose-water, allowed to soak in for an hour, prevents premature wrinkling. Above all she recommended the special brides' bath (see page 93), used regularly in rich families with a special maid to attend to it, a treatment which she had until she was twenty-one.

Cocoa Butter Ointment

Mary recommends rubbing a cocoa-butter stick from the chemist into the bags under the eyes. Or make this simple ointment.

25g (1oz) cocoa butter	*25g (1oz) lanolin*
1 teaspoon rose-water	

Melt the butter and lanolin together in a bowl over hot water. Stir in the rose-water, remove from the heat and stir until cool. Use two or three times a day under the eyes.

Mary also extolled the virtues of *Rosa rubiginosa* oil for dry and ageing skin. It helps smooth out wrinkles and is also excellent for scarred skin, and those brown spots that come with age.

A woman born in Shropshire told me that her grandmother used to drink comfrey tea (see page 123) regularly, and she had hardly any wrinkles. Nettle tea had the same effect, she claimed, and a face pack of pulped apples keeps the skin firm and helps keep away wrinkles.

Anti-wrinkle Cream

A softening, aromatic cream which, using the master recipe as a base, enriches the skin and leaves it smooth. It sets hard but softens on contact with the skin.

7g (¼oz) beeswax	*1 tablespoon infusion*
15g (½oz) cocoa butter	*(see page 68) of your chosen*
1 teaspoon honey	*anti-wrinkle herb (see below)*
2 tablespoons almond oil	*3 drops of honeysuckle or other*
2 teaspoons wheatgerm oil	*essential oil*

Follow the directions for the master recipe on page 68.

Anti-wrinkle Herbs

Make infusions (see page 68) with any of the following: comfrey, elderflowers, fennel, honeysuckle, houseleek, lady's mantle, lime blossom, marshmallow.

Anti-wrinkle Wash

Make a strong infusion (see page 68) of poppy flowers. Spray on to the face liberally with a fine atomizer before applying the anti-wrinkle cream above.

FACIALS

In some parts of the world face masks serve a double purpose: for instance, women in Mozambique wear herbal face paint that also protects their skin. Facials are nourishing for the skin. They literally 'feed your face', drawing out impurities and improving the circulation. They contain either egg (yolk for dry skin, white for oily), banana or honey as binders. A few drops of cider vinegar help the acid balance of the skin. Facials are also relaxing since you have to lie down quietly for 20 minutes!

Two useful tips from Mary, based on long experience: firstly, always take out contact lenses or false teeth before you start a facial treatment; secondly, if you apply the facial through a layer of fine gauze it makes the process neater and cleaner – you simply peel it off at the end of the treatment, instead of having a mess to deal with. Buy fine gauze from a chemist, cut out an oval quite a bit larger than your face, and cut small holes for the eyes and nostrils.

You need 1–2 tablespoons of any mixture below for a face pack. You can store leftovers in the fridge and use up within a week.

To Apply a Facial

Pull the hair back from the face. Clean the skin with cold water or a cold cream. Lay the gauze over the face and pat the prepared facial on to it with your fingertips or with cotton wool pads. Lie down and relax for 20 minutes to allow it to soak in and take effect. Don't bother to answer the phone or the door. Peel off the gauze, and refresh the skin with your favourite flower water (see page 94).

Cucumber

Cucumber has the same acid-alkaline balance as the skin and has a positive but neutral effect on the skin. Peeled cucumber is an excellent addition to facials, or just rub a piece of peeled cucumber over the face to cool it. Rinse off with tepid water 10 minutes later. Drink a tumbler of cucumber juice every day, made in a juicer, to clear the skin. Or just lay slices of peeled cucumber over the face while lying down, and relax for 10 minutes: deliciously cool.

Buttermilk

This is good for oily skins. It is rich in calcium and protein and added to a few mashed strawberries, is a healthy drink.

buttermilk   *1 cucumber, peeled*

Wash your face in cold water and dry thoroughly. Apply a thin layer of buttermilk and allow to dry for 15-20 minutes. Slice the cucumber, layer over the face and relax for 10 minutes.

You can also try buttermilk followed by strawberries, which is very good for oily skins. Apply in the same way. Strawberries have a mildly bleaching effect and help remove discoloration and blemishes from the skin.

Brewers' Yeast

Brewers' yeast moistened with rose-water is an excellent addition to any facial for oily skin.

Carrot Facial

Mary remembers her mother making this mixture. The large amounts of vitamin A in carrots are healing for the skin. Either juice two large carrots in a juicer, or soak 2 tablespoons of grated carrots in 1 tablespoon safflower oil. Add a few drops of cider vinegar or lemon juice. To bind, add 1 tablespoon crushed banana, or honey, or a beaten egg yolk.

Grapes

This facial helps restore the natural acidity of the skin, especially when the skin has been dried out by too much sun. Grape juice is a good flush for the system and improves skin tone generally. This recipe comes from a friend of mine who lived in Italy for many years.

100g (4oz) seedless grapes, mashed
1 tablespoon honey
1 egg yolk, beaten (or egg white for oily skin)

Mix all together and apply as a mask.

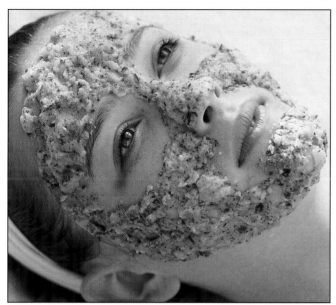

Take time out for a facial and relax. Find a quiet place, close the door – and recuperate.

Avocado

Avocado is rich in fats and vitamins and Mary recommends it highly for a mature skin. The make-up of avocado oil is the nearest in nature to that of our human skin, and its buttery richness replaces the natural oils lost on washing and weathering. It leaves the skin feeling smooth and velvety. You can also use this as a body rub before a warm bath.

2 tablespoons mashed avocado
1 teaspoon honey
3 drops cider vinegar

Mix all together well and add some sesame oil if you wish. Apply as a facial, see left.

Coconut

Rafath traditionally uses coconut 'milk' to moisturize and enrich her skin.

Pour 150 ml (¼ pint) boiling water over 50g (2oz) desiccated coconut and leave to stand until it reaches room temperature. Strain off and use as a thin mask, washing it off after it has dried. Or add 1 teaspoon to a facial made up of honey, ground almonds, egg yolk and cider vinegar.

Tahini

This makes a brilliant face mask: it feeds the skin, tightens the face and brings vitality to the skin. Its protein nourishes and its oiliness lubricates.

Mix some tahini with a few drops of cider vinegar, and leave on the skin for 10 minutes. Rinse off with warm water mixed with a few more drops of cider vinegar or lemon juice.

Oatmeal

This acts as a cleansing scrub which removes dead and dry skin, and nourishes the pores. Mary suggests soaking the oatmeal in orange-flower water first.

1 egg yolk   *1 tablespoon honey*
1 tablespoon fine oatmeal   *1 tablespoon sesame or almond oil*

Mix together and apply to a clean face. Allow to dry for 20 minutes, then rinse off with warm water. Wipe the face with a flower water to finish.

Alternatively, beat up an egg white, mix with a little fine oatmeal and apply to a clean face.

Apricot

This is a favourite of mine, more like cooking than beauty care. I use unsulphured apricots (and eat one or two as I go along, to increase the effect of the treatment!).

Mash or blend fresh or dried, soaked apricots and mix with olive oil to form a paste. Apply and leave for 20 minutes. Great for dry skin, and a source of vitamin A.

Almond

A woman I met in San Francisco got this recipe from her Mexican maid. I tried it and my skin loved it. Almonds soften the skin, cleanse it with their abrasive action and nourish it with protein.

25g (⅛oz) ground almonds
2 tablespoons rose-water
3 tablespoons almond or olive oil
1 egg white for oily skins, 1 egg yolk for dry skins

Mix the ingredients together and apply.

An old-fashioned mustard foot-bath is a great reviver.

BATHS AND BODY RUBS

Soaking in a warm bath is a great restorer. I love to add herbs for special effects. The beauty of herbal baths is that they cost very little, they stimulate the pores of the skin, yet are soothing, rejuvenating and pleasurable.

Herbs for the Bath

The most practical way to make a herb bath is to put the herbs into a muslin bag and tie it around the tap so that the water runs through it. Add a little oatmeal to soften the water, and give smoothness to the skin. Squeeze thoroughly once the bath is run, to get the ultimate extraction.

You can also infuse about 100g (4oz) fresh leaves or flowers in 1.2 litres (2 pints) boiling water. Pour the water on to the herb and leave to steep for 10 minutes. Then strain it off and add 600ml (1 pint) to the bath water.

Rosemary: To bath in rosemary makes the old young again, so they say, so either use a bag, as above, or steep 50g (2oz) rosemary leaves in 600ml (1 pint) boiling water for 10 minutes.

Add to the bath water and soak in it. Or simmer a handful of dried rosemary leaves in 600ml (1 pint) of wine for 20 minutes. Cool, strain and add to the bath.

Balm leaves relieve nervous tension and insomnia.

English walnut leaves are excellent for rheumatism, gout – and sweaty feet! This is according to an American friend.

Camomile flowers are extremely good for skin problems, varicose veins, and ulcers.

Elderflowers cool sunburnt skin.

Blackberry (young leaves and shoots) makes a superb tonic after a long winter.

Other Recommended Mixtures:

• Camomile, rosemary and lavender.

• Sage, fennel and yarrow.

• Peppermint, rosemary and horsetail.

• Thyme and lavender.

• Nettle and dandelion.

Baths to Restore Energy

An Australian friend swears by pouring a cup of cider vinegar into a tepid bath. It will also soften rough skin. Mary advises Epsom salts in the bath to relieve aches and pains – or Dead Sea salts if you can get them.

Footbaths

Footbaths are surprisingly revitalizing and have the effect of restoring a tired body. Soak your feet in a warm herbal footbath then massage them with 1 teaspoon of wheatgerm oil mixed with 3 drops of essential oil of rosemary or lavender. Mary suggests rubbing coarse salt on to the feet to remove the dead skin first.

The best herbs to infuse (see page 68) for the feet are: elderberries, mugwort, nettles, peppermint, pine needles, rosemary, sage and yarrow. Soak the feet for 10 minutes.

Old-fashioned Mustard Footbath

Mary's Scottish grandmother passed this down to the family. Put 225g (8oz) ground mustard in a cloth bag. Place in a pan with enough water to cover and bring to the boil. Boil for 10 minutes. Add to a hot footbath for colds, flu, and so on.

For Tired and Aching Feet

An old English country remedy:

50g (2oz) fresh marigold leaves
1.2 litres (2 pints) boiling water

Pour the boiling water on to the leaves. Cover and leave to cool. Strain into the footbath. An infusion of lavender is equally good.

Horsetail Infusion for Tired and Aching Limbs

One of the best-known footbaths is made from this common weed.

1.2 litres (2 pints) water
50g (2oz) dried horsetail

Pour the water on to the horsetail and leave to soak for 2 hours. Then bring to the boil and simmer for 15 minutes. Strain into the warm footbath.

Bath oils

I add 10–12 drops of a favourite essential oil to my bath once it has run. You can add sandalwood oil to 150ml (¼ pint) base oil – almond is good – to give the bath an exotic fragrance. Rub the oiliness into the skin as you wash. Using treated (sulphonated) castor oil instead of almond leaves no ring around the bath.

Lavender Essence for the Bath

From a household hints book of the early 1900s. The name lavender comes from the Latin *lavare*, to wash.

Infuse 3 handfuls of lavender flowers in 300ml (½ pint) spirits of wine (pure alcohol, see page 66) for 3 days, then strain. To the liquid add a few drops of oil of lavender, 30ml (1fl oz) orange-flower water and 60ml (2fl oz) distilled water. Shake thoroughly, and pour into a narrow-necked bottle. Use sparingly.

Body Rubs

Body rubs cleanse the pores, getting rid of dead cells while at the same time nourishing and moisturizing the skin. Indian brides go through days of ritual massaging with coconut or mustard oil before their wedding, plus treatments with cream and saffron or turmeric to make the skin radiant. Gram flour mixed with cream is rubbed in to take away any hard or dead skin, and then they have a complete bath in olive oil. These two rubs are less exotic but still bliss.

Take a cup of coarse sea salt and moisten it with a little cider vinegar. Prepare a cup of almond oil (or you can use safflower, olive, soy or sesame). Run the bath and when it it ready rub your body all over with the oil. Put some salt on to a flannel and rub it over the oil layer. Massage well to remove dead or rough skin. Then soak in your bath.

Mix 100ml (4fl oz) avocado oil with 1 tablespoon each of honey, egg yolk and mashed banana to bind, and a few drops of cider vinegar. Add some pinhead oatmeal for a rough and stimulating rub, or fine oatmeal for a softer effect. If you only have rolled oats in the house, process them in a blender.

Rub into the body, massaging well, and let it soak in for 10 minutes at least to moisturize the skin. Wash off in a deep, warm bath.

If you suffer from cellulite, massage the areas with rosemary and geranium essential oils, or infusions, after the bath.

SWEET WATERS

Use flower waters as skin toners. If you apply them to the face before a moisturizer, this will contain the flower water and increase its effect. My grandmother used to use a mixture of witch-hazel and rose-water with a little glycerine added. Flower waters used to be put into finger-bowls at table, for dipping fingers into between courses.

Distilled flower waters, used in cosmetic care and for fragrance around the home, are best bought ready-made: lavender water, rose-water and witch-hazel are readily available from chemists and deserve a place in the bathroom cupboard. You can make your own elderflower water, but it is perishable and needs to be kept in the fridge. It tones and refines the skin.

Elderflower Water

1 handful fresh elderflowers   600ml (1 pint) boiling water

Put the flowers into a jug, crush them gently and pour the boiling water over them. Cover and leave to steep overnight. Strain through coffee filter paper into a bottle, and store in the fridge. Add a tablespoon of vodka to make it last longer, or a teaspoon of tincture of benzoin to preserve it.

You can use this method to make any flower water.

Jasmine makes the most exquisite flower water – excellent for a dry, sensitive skin – and the aroma is wonderful.
Quince blossom is wonderful too, refining the pores of the skin and whitening it.

Orange-flower Water

This was highly esteemed by Marie Antoinette, who found that it refined and lightened her sallow skin.

*1 heaped tablespoon dried orange   90ml (3fl oz) boiling water
blossom, available from herbalists
and good apothecaries*

Place the blossom in a small bowl and pour on the water. Cover and leave for 15 minutes. Strain off the water, pressing the flowers

well. Bottle, and keep in the fridge. Add a little vodka to make it keep longer.

Lavender Water

Lavender is wonderfully soothing and calming for inflamed skin, and an excellent toner for normal skin. This recipe comes from a *Commonplace Book*, dated 1813.

*1.2 litres (2 pints) pure alcohol   1½ teaspoons essence of ambergris
1 tablespoon oil of lavender   5–6 drops musk
1 tablespoon essence of bergamot*

Put all the ingredients into a bottle and shake well. Store for 3 months before use.

A simpler version is to mix 30ml (1fl oz) oil of lavender with 900ml (1½ pints) pure alcohol. Shake well.

Hungary Water

Used by Queen Elizabeth of Hungary, who was renowned for her great beauty even at the age of 80.

*600ml (1 pint) pure alcohol   1½ teaspoons essence of ambergris
30ml (1fl oz) oil of rosemary   Finely grated peel of 1 orange and 1 lemon*

Place all the ingredients in a bottle and shake well. Seal and leave for 24 hours. Shake daily for a month.

A Sweet Water

This wonderful water tones a lacklustre skin, and you can also use it as an aftershave. Or just inhale it – its aroma lifts the spirits!

Take Damask Roses at discretion, Basil, Sweet marjoram, Lavender, Walnut Leafs, of each two handfuls, Rosemary one handful, a little Balm, Cloves, Cinnamon, one ounce, Bay Leaf, Rosemary tops, Limon and Orange Pills*, of each a few; pour upon these as much white wine as will conveniently wet them, and let them infuse for ten or twelve days; then distil it off.   Sir Kenelm Digby, Receipts 1668

*Use 2 tablespoons of finely grated orange and lemon peel

'Hungary Water' was invented for the legendary Hungarian beauty Queen Elizabeth who continued to attract lovers well into her old age.

Facial Steams

Gently fragrant, facial steams cleanse the pores deeply, and soften and moisturize the skin. Mary recommends these as being particularly good for blemished and oily skins. Don't use them on very dry, sensitive skins, and avoid them if you are asthmatic. Cover the hair and clean the face. Place 2 tablespoons of your chosen herb in a bowl and pour on 600ml (1 pint) of boiling water. Hold your face 20–30cm (8–12in) above the water with a towel over your head so that the rising steam can penetrate the pores. Stay there for 8–10 minutes. Allow your face to cool, then wipe with a cold flannel dipped in a flower water of your choice.

The Herbs

Choose from lime, sage and peppermint, camomile, yarrow and lady's mantle (for acne), basil, sweet pea, elderflower, marigold flower, nasturtium, cornflower, lavender flower or fennel.

HEALING
HERBS

The art of using herbs to cure all manner of ailments goes back to the beginnings of civilization when man was intricately connected to the natural world in his everyday life, and in tune with the cycles and rhythms of the turning year. He would observe how animals would select certain leaves to cure themselves, and how sick people would instinctively eat particular plant foods. The Bedouin mother would wash her newborn child in camel's urine: today's biologists have found this to be a protection from several sorts of infection. In the days before penicillin the Canadian lumberjack knew that the mould of bad bread was the best thing for an axe wound. And people used herbs to cure ills and maintain health. Over the centuries a vast body of wisdom has accumulated, both oral and written, some of which still survives in rural parts of the world, and a great deal of which has been authenticated by scientists.

The earliest roots of herbalism come from country people, often women, living in simple rural communities and passing on their wisdom informally down the generations. It was only later that scholars picked up on and disseminated this knowledge by means of the written word, at about the time that 'physic' gardens came into their own. There is fragmentary evidence of ancient Egyptian 'medicinal' gardens, which were further developed in Greece under the influence of Aristotle and Hippocrates, but they virtually disappeared until the Middle Ages in Europe, when  herbal medicine was almost entirely practised by monks. They were the first great practising herbalists, growing 'physic herbs' in their infirmary gardens to supply the poor and the sick with medicines in the monastery hospital. Herbs were regarded as holy because they were given by God to cure our ills. The infirmary garden was small, enclosed, and sheltered, and typically would include the planting of many foreign herbs brought back by the Crusaders from Egypt and Syria. It was a peaceful place, enclosed by thick hedges or high walls, sweet-smelling and tranquil, to restore the soul as well as the body.

The first formal physic gardens were what we now know as botanical gardens. The first one in western Europe – and in the world – was set up in Pisa (1543), followed by Padua and Florence in 1545. Bologna, Leiden, Montpelier, Strasbourg, Uppsala, Paris, Amsterdam, Oxford and Edinburgh followed over the next 100 years. They were given various names: 'Hortus medicus', 'Jardin des Plantes', and 'Physick garden'. Here grew plants for medicinal, educational  and scientific purposes, for students of medicine and apothecaries to use like a library.

One of the world's most famous physic gardens, although not the oldest, is at Chelsea, planted by the Apothecaries Company in 1683. Linnaeus, the great eighteenth-century Swedish botanist and explorer who created a uniform system for the botanical naming of plants, walked there, and another of its many claims to fame was that it had the first hothouse in England. Its four acres are still there to be used for the ongoing purposes of education and science: the learning gleaned from this research can be found in herbals and pharmacopoeia, ancient and modern.

Culpeper assigned certain flowers and herbs to each sun-sign.

HERBAL WISDOM AND ASTROLOGY

Those men and women skilled in applying the healing qualities of plants have always held an honoured place in their societies: many were also priests or priestesses acting as mediums for the gods as they dispensed their mysterious and magic medicines the world over. It is thought that a Chinese emperor composed a herbal around 2700 BC, but Chinese herbals have only relatively recently been translated for Western use. Indian herbal wisdom dates back to the Vedas, written around 1500–1200 BC, and the practice of Ayurvedic medicine has continued to this day in India and elsewhere. The development of medical studies in ancient Egypt and Mesopotamia spread to the countries of the eastern Mediterranean, to Persia and Armenia, and thence to ancient Greece. They took root in Europe and thence travelled to the

New World where the native Indians had already independently evolved their own herbal practices, which they claimed came through dreams and intuitions, and the word of the 'little people.' Russia had its 'wolf-men' who dispensed herbal medicine, the Celts their Druids. An Aztec herbal translated in 1522 shows quite independent evidence of herbal medicine in South America from very early days.

In Europe, the systems of Aristotle and Theophrastus laid the foundations for the great herbal of the first true medical botanist, Dioscorides, in the first century AD. His *Materia Medica* became the model for the herbals of the Anglo-Saxons and the medieval monks. St Hildegard of Bingen, the German visionary, wrote a herbal in the eleventh century based on local folk-cures, as well as on the received word of God. At about this time, Arabic medicine, with its proximity to medicinal plants from the east, culminated in the work of Avicenna. Out of sixteenth-century Germany came the herbals of Brunfels, Bock and Fuchs, from Holland those of Dodoens, L'Ecluse and L'Obel, and Mattioli's from Italy. The Renaissance had a profound effect on medical knowledge, producing the famous herbals of Turner and John Gerard in England. The most famous herbalist of them all, Nicholas Culpeper, was also an astrologer.

Astrology

From Babylonian times men and animals, vegetables and minerals were thought to be under the dominion of the planets. The oldest astrologers taught that the seven known planets (Sun, Moon, Mercury, Venus, Mars, Saturn and Jupiter) all had influence over plant life and that they had their own herbs, trees and flowers. Both

Hippocrates and Galen advised physicians to be instructed in astronomy, and in primitive cultures the moon in particular is acknowledged as an influence in certain diseases. Many of the great herbalists have combined the profession of herbalist with astrologer. 'He must know the mathematical sciences, and especially astrologie', wrote Culpeper's contemporary, the seventeenth-century Italian herbalist Giambattista della Porta.

Above all things next to grammar a physician must surely have his Astronomye, to know how, when and at what time every medicine ought to be administered. 16th-century physician

Culpeper assigned to each herb its ruling planet. The attribution of plants to the signs of the Zodiac is one of the lighter sides of astrology: the theory goes that the vibrations or force fields emitted by particular plants are compatible with, and can have beneficial effects on, the health of people born under the ruling of that planet.

Aries (Mars): thistles, nettles, brambles, mustard, onion, peppers, geranium, honeysuckle, witch-hazel, rosemary, marjoram, garlic, horseradish, cowslip.

Taurus (Venus): damask roses, violets, primroses, vine, rose, poppy, foxglove, mint, thyme, tansy, coltsfoot, lovage.

Gemini (Mercury): lily of the valley, speedwell, lavender, mild aromatic herbs (parsley, dill, fennel, caraway, marjoram).

Cancer (Moon): waterlilies and all water plants, forget-me-nots, saxifrages, white poppy, mouse-ear, acanthus, wild flowers, agrimony, balm, daisies, lettuce, cucumber.

Leo (Sun): sunflowers, dahlias, St John's wort, saffron, rue, marigold, rosemary, borage, camomile.

Virgo (Mercury): lily of the valley, speedwell, lavender, mild aromatic herbs (as Gemini), small brightly coloured flowers, southernwood, savory, fennel, valerian.

Libra (Venus): large damask roses, violets, primroses, vine, blue flowers, dandelion, yarrow, pennyroyal.

Scorpio (Mars): thistles, nettles, brambles, onion, mustard, peppers, dark red flowers such as rhododendrons, basil, tarragon, barberry.

Sagittarius (Jupiter): red roses (not damask), meadowsweet, jasmine, houseleek, asparagus, pinks, dandelion, sage, samphire, chervil.

Capricorn (Saturn): pansy, henbane, hemlock, deadly nightshade, onions, ivy, comfrey, red beets, sorrel, Solomon's seal.

Aquarius (Uranus): orchid, golden rain, elderberry, fumitory, mullein, barley.

Pisces (Jupiter and Neptune): red roses (not damask), meadowsweet, jasmine, houseleek, waterlily, fig, bilberry, rose hip, lungwort.

APOTHECARIES AND STILL-ROOMS

The late Middle Ages saw the emergence of the apothecary as somewhat more than a quack (he was originally a simple shopkeeper who traded in drugs and herbs) and above the ranking of 'grocer' with which he was associated in the trade companies. Apothecaries all over Europe began to establish their own physic gardens to serve as a link between horticulture and medicine, where they grew their own medicinal herbs. They also purchased herbs and roots collected from the countryside by 'green men and women', and imported drugs and spices from abroad. English apothecaries succeeded in setting up the Worshipful Company of Apothecaries in 1617 which allowed them to prescribe and diagnose without reference to a physician, a practice which remained legal until 1886.

A typical seventeeth-century apothecary's shop had walls lined with wooden chests of drawers in miniature, the shelves lined with bottles and jars of all colours and descriptions, weighing scales, pots and pans, boxes and burners. In such a place, between the fifteenth and seventeenth centuries, the apothecary would diagnose his patients, then make up and sell the required herbal remedies.

Distillation

The practice of distillation was refined in Arabia in the fourth century with the Hermetic science of alchemy, and these practitioners eventually became expert in the distillation of aromatic waters and alcohol. The legend goes that a doctor was called away to a patient in the middle of a meal. When he returned, the plate which had covered his food was beaded with moisture: he pondered on this, and did the first experiments in distillation.

A still consists of a retort in which substances are heated, a condenser in which the vapours are condensed, and a receiver in which the condensed vapours are collected. 'It is to be understood that distilling is nothing else but a purifying of the gross from the subtle, the subtle from the gross, each separately from the other to the intent that the corruptible shall be made incorruptible and to make the material immaterial.' So begins the first great treatise on distillation written in 1500 by Brunschwig, a physician of Strasbourg. A seventeenth-century recipe describes a water distilled from the

flowers of jasmine, honeysuckle, violet, and lily 'to retain the smell of their flowers'. Distillation today is chiefly from leaves, barks and woods, with oils of lavender, rosemary, mint, rose-water and orange-flower water being distilled from the flowers.

The Still-room

In Europe, while the cottager had to make do with simple preparations from a homemade still, using herbs from the hedgerows and flowers from his cottage garden, the rich man in his country house would as often as not have a still-room where the still-room maid had dominion. She ruled over the herb garden and orchard, ensuring that both were harvested at the right time, in tune with the

phases of the moon and with the correct charms, rites and ceremonies. Her knowledge of medicinal herbs was sufficient to provide the household with simple remedies, and her skills extended to aromatic vinegars, syrups and conserves, aromatic candies and perfumes. Her pot-pourri would scent the elegant sitting-rooms, her oil of roses soothe the baby's skin after bathing. Her beauty lotions from 'the toilet of Flora' as the Elizabethans called it, beautified the skin of the lady of the house, her homemade wines furnished the servants' table. Her job it was to strew bedchambers and privies with aromatic herbs and flowers, and to make posies of herbs and flowers for the lord and lady to carry in the street, protecting them from frightful smells and infectious diseases. These were even carried to church, to ward off any noxious smells from the common people and to refresh the brain during the service.

She would undoubtedly have had a herbal on the shelf, alongside jars of spring water, pots and funnels, pestle and mortar and a stag's horn for mixing. The still-room was a fascinating, fragrant place with bunches of herbs and flowers hanging to dry, and rose petals spread out to make scented bags, like this one from an eighteenth-century commonplace book.

A Bagge to Smelle unto for Melancholie or to Cause One to Sleep

Take drie rose leves keep them close in a glasse which will keep them sweet and then take pouder of mynte, powder of cloves in a grosse pouder, and putte the same to the Rose leves thanne putte all these togyther in a bagge and take that to bedde with you and it wyll cause you to sleepe and it is goode to smelle unto at other tymes.

NATURAL FRAGRANCES FOR THE HOME

Part of my childhood was spent in a beautiful house in Cambridge, the Master's Lodge of one of the colleges. My mother had a keen eye for the elegant and extended her skills to home-made aromatics, made from the flowers the college gardeners grew for us in the herbaceous walled garden. I used to help her dry the petals and herbs, and loved the days spent mixing the fragrances to make what seemed like magical combinations to scent the house. These are some of the recipes we made together.

Pomanders

These were traditionally threaded on a cord and carried about to ward off infection, or to protect from the evil smells of the street. Sometimes carried in a perforated box of ivory, silver or even gold, they were worn as a fashion accessory.

Pomanders are a lovely way to scent a room, or to perfume a wardrobe, and are also for keeping moths away from cupboards where clothes and fabrics are stored.

> *1 orange*
> *Good quality cloves, with the heads intact*
> *Orris root* (Iris germanica)
> *Ground cinnamon*

Stick the orange full of cloves, leaving a small space between each one since the orange will shrink as it dries. Use a fine knitting needle to make the holes.

Mix the orris root and cinnamon and roll the finished pomander in the mixture, rubbing it in well. Place in an airing cupboard or warm dry place for 2 weeks, then tie with a ribbon and hang up.

Sweet Bags

My mother used to perfume the linen cupboard with these bags, which also keep moths away. You can also hang these over a chair,

A pomander.

Pot-pourri.

or loop them on to clothes-hangers. Use any combination of flowers or herbs (see Pot-pourri below), plus a few drops of essential oil. My mother's favourite was dried lemon verbena leaves. Make up small bags with muslin or fine linen, attaching a length of ribbon to hang them by.

Plain lavender bags are hard to beat, too. I make them with little squares of wild silk and tie them with ribbons. They keep their scent for a year. Once you have stripped the stalks, pack them into old stockings and use to scent the airing or linen cupboard.

Herb Pot-pourri

Use a mixture of peppermint, sweet cicely, sage, basil, rosemary, angelica, lemon thyme, lemon balm, red bergamot, lovage, tarragon, marjoram or rose geranium leaves, all dried.
Add ground coriander and nutmeg for a highly aromatic mixture, and proceed as above.

Herb Cushions

Hop pillows are famous for helping insomniacs – King George III couldn't sleep without one. Lavender is excellent too, and rosemary, they say, keeps bad dreams away. You can also use peppermint, sage or lemon balm, plus a choice of dill, marjoram,

thyme, lemon thyme, tarragon, woodruff, rose geranium, angelica, rosemary, lemon verbena or bergamot.

Dry the leaves (see page 121). Make small pillows 20cm (8in) square, using a porous natural fabric such as fine linen or cotton, and stuff with the mixture.

Flower Pot-pourri

Bowls of pot-pourri add elegance as well as fragrance to a room. You can use scented petals, leaves, flowers and herbs: orange blossom, lemon verbena, honeysuckle, lily of the valley, stocks, lavender, clove pinks, rose petals, sweet geranium, bergamot, violets, jasmine, lemon peel, rosemary and bay leaves are all excellent. Dry them on newspaper or muslin in a warm place such as the airing cupboard until they are brittle – about a week to 10 days.

1.2 litres (2 pints) dried flowers
25g (1oz) dried orris root or benzoin powder (fixative)
1 teaspoon ground spice such as nutmeg, mace, cloves, cinnamon
1 tablespoon whole spices such as cloves, cinnamon, mace, cumin, allspice
10–12 drops essential oils of your choice such as lavender, rosemary, geranium, lemon, and so on

Put the dried flowers into a bowl between layers of fixative. Add the ground and whole spices and finally drop in the essential oils. Turn by hand once or twice per week. The mixture will last for up to two years.

Incense

Not really incense, but it fills the room with a memorable and exotic scent – flowery and spicy with all the mystery of the East.

12g (½oz) each dried lavender flowers, rose petals and lemon verbena
12g (½oz) each whole cloves and stick cinnamon, pounded in a mortar
25g (1oz) orris root powder
12g (½oz) gum benzoin
8–10 drops each essential oils of sweet orange, clove, bergamot and rose

Combine the dry ingredients and mix well. Sprinkle the oils over and mix again. Store in a dark place for 2 weeks, covered, for the scents to combine. Then place the mixture in a metal container on top of a radiator. As it heats gently it will perfume the room.

CURES FROM THE KITCHEN

'You are what you eat', a popular aphorism in many cultures, is ascribed to Chinese wisdom, and there are numerous foods which can double up as medicines. The obvious connection between what you put into your body and how your health is affected is the basis of Indian Ayurvedic medicine, but this philosophy appears independently in other cultures too. Magdalena, a teacher from the Nahuatl tribe in North-East Mexico, was highly respected in her community as a powerful healer. Her three 'pillars of health' were onions, lemons and garlic – for prevention as well as for cure. She used onions to purify the blood, their sulphur compounds stimulate the digestive system and their natural antibiotics maintain healthy gut flora, increasing the body's resistance against disease. The antidioxant properties of lemons have a similar effect. They help digestion, are antiseptic and detoxifying, and improve the circulation. Garlic, famous throughout history for its beneficial effects, is powerfully antibiotic and antiseptic. It has been found to reduce cholesterol levels, is expectorant and decongestant, and it improves the digestion. Magdalena's personal panacea was to eat several cloves of garlic, raw, before breakfast on an empty stomach!

My Indian friend Rafath's aunt lent me her Ayurvedic 'bible', well-marked with all her favourite remedies, some of which are included here. There is a wealth of everyday wisdom from the Ayurvedic tradition, which is grounded in herbs, spices and food plants. So comprehensive is it that it took the author 16 years to complete his book, and in his introduction he quotes Socrates: 'diet is health and diet is medicine', and informs his readers that the Greek word for diet means 'way of living'.

This tradition is rich in everyday remedies: among the simplest are using vinegar for shingles and impetigo, and washing ulcers in warm tea. For nerves, eat an apple with honey and milk daily; for cramps in the calf muscles, drinking half a teaspoon of salt in a glass of water three times daily. If you want to lose weight, drink the fresh juice of a lime mixed with a glass of cold water and sweetened with honey every morning on an empty stomach for two months – plus eating a low-calorie diet. Alternatively, eat two tomatoes every morning on an empty stomach. Eating a clove a day increases longevity – and sitting regularly under the shade of a nutmeg tree cures obesity!

Headaches Rafath's mother would make a tea with cardamom, fennel and lemongrass, put a mask over her eyes and lie down in a quiet room. Alternatively, make this ginger poultice, which will relieve muscle tension, as well as soothe and cure. Make a paste with 2 tablespoons ground ginger and a little water, and warm it gently in a saucepan. Spread this on to a pad made with lint and cotton wool, and apply to the forehead, before lying down in a quiet place.

Coughs and Colds Rafath's family cure was weak tea with ginger and honey, and lemon added if it was a chesty cough. Ginger is antispasmodic and so relieves the urge to cough, and it is a warming herb much used in colds. For the early stages of a cold or bronchitis, take 1 teaspoon onion juice with 1 tablespoon honey 3 times daily. You can chew a clove (they are antispasmodic and antiseptic) with a crystal of salt to relieve throat irritation.

Hippocrates recommends vinegar as a decongestant to

treat coughs: try a couple of teaspoons in hot water. No bugs can survive the high acetic acid content of vinegar. Alternatively, make this garlic juice: cut several cloves of garlic into thin slices, cover with honey and leave for 2–3 hours. Take the resulting juice by the teaspoon at intervals during the day. Alternatively, make this with chopped raw onion.

Sore Throats

For a chesty cough my old nanny used to administer vinegar, honey and brown sugar heated together. Sometimes she would add cloves, other times garlic. The commonest remedy of all for coughs and colds is a simple mixture of lemon and honey, I tablespoon of each, in a cup of warm water. For the grown-ups, add whisky.

Dominic's great-aunt Beryl who lives in Greenwich pre-scribed frozen grapes for a sore throat. He reported that they were delicious, and also had the desired anaesthetic effect.

A gargle of salt water is an ancient home cure for a sore throat.

Flu

From Ayurvedic wisdom, for flu and rhinitis add a pinch of pepper and honey to powdered cinnamon, add hot water and sip. Pepper is expectorant, and cinnamon a 'warming' spice which has long been used for chills and colds. A remedy from Wales for bronchitis is to rub goose fat into the chest and cover it with a red flannel.

Chilblains

A Russian friend told me that her family had always put cayenne pepper into their socks during the terrible Russian winters. A Chinese woman uses ginger. Cayenne has long been used in the Americas, South-East Asia, India and Europe for its warming, stimulating effect. A simple ointment of base oil with cayenne or chilli pepper stimulates the blood flow and is excellent for chilblains as well as for lumbago and muscular pain.

Arthritis

Rafath's aunt rubbed mustard oil into her arthritic hands. This cure is also used on horses, both in India and the West. Mustard is extremely effective at stimulating the circulation. Also from her aunt's canon: to reduce pain and stiffness in painful joints, use equal measures of lime juice and castor oil, and drink 1 teaspoon of this in warm water with honey. The purging effects of castor oil clear the body of toxins.

One of the best-known cures for arthritis is the cider vinegar and honey recipe on page 111.

Earache

Rafath's mother would warm some olive oil, prick a clove of garlic with a pin, soak it in the oil, place it in the ear and plug with cotton wool. A woman from the Fens in East Anglia, a complete stranger to Ayurvedic medicine, recommended an almost identical remedy, but made with a baked onion. Or, Rafath continued, use onion sprinkled with turmeric and heated on a chapati-griddle.

Stomach Problems

A friend in her nineties who lived in South Africa for many years tells how when she was poorly as a child she was given vinegar and salt to make her sick, to clear up infection and clear the system of toxins. One teaspoon of mustard powder in a cup of hot water is emetic, and useful in cases of food poisoning. Likewise a solution of salt. Ayurvedic wisdom offers drinking coconut water (the clear liquid from inside the shell) for biliousness. And drink lemon or lime juice in water with salt and pepper for stomachache.

Oats are soothing to the digestive tract and help gastritis, constipation, diverticulitis and irritable bowel syndrome. Ginger, with its soothing effect on the digestive system, is ideal for travel sickness and has proved exceptionally useful in early-morning sickness. Drink ginger tea, or chew a little of the root – or if all else fails ginger biscuits or ginger ale go a long way to helping.

Simplest of all for regular stomachache is a cup of tea: PG stands for pre-gestive, and 'Typhoo' is Chinese for 'doctor'.

Hangovers Red hot chillies encourage the body to release its natural painkillers, the endomorphins. A Californian remedy is 3 chillis blended with 500ml (17fl oz) tomato juice and a squirt of soy sauce.

The natural sugars and complex carbohydrates of this remedy from an African doctor help increase the calming brain chemical serotonin: blend a banana with 500ml (17fl oz) soya milk and 2 tablespoons of fruit concentrate. Chill for 30 minutes and drink up.

Jaundice Mr Leeroy, now in his eighties, lives on Harbour Island in the Bahamas. 'Everything that grows on Mother Earth is healing to the nation', he declares. Diagnosed as being dangerously ill with jaundice he defied death by treating himself with a mixture of watermelon seeds, sweet cicely, yellow limes, baking powder and water. He drank a mugful every three hours and was cured in three days.

Urinary Tract Infections Cranberry juice is a scientifically proven remedy in the prevention and treatment of urinary tract infections. For generations North Americans have used it for cystitis and kidney complaints. Research suggests that cranberries contain a substance that stops the infectious bacteria from clinging to the cells that line the urinary tract and bladder, preventing them from multiplying. Recent Israeli research has found that blueberry juice has a similar effect.

Blend cranberries in a food processor and add a little water to bring to a liquid consistency. Stir well and drink three times a day.

Arteriosclerosis Russians recommend that everyone over forty should eat a grated raw potato before breakfast to delay arteriosclerosis.

Onions are thought to bring down blood pressure. They contain an antiseptic oil which substantially lowers blood cholesterol and this reduces the risk of coronary heart disease. One tablespoon of chopped onion per day will suffice, raw or cooked – the oil is not destroyed on cooking.

Oats likewise reduces cholesterol by means of the soluble fibre binding to the cholesterol and causing it to be excreted rather than reabsorbed. So eat lots of porridge!

Small Wounds and Cuts Garlic is highly antibiotic and combats infections of all kinds. Eat a lot of it, raw or cooked. The ancient Egyptians gave it to the workers who were building the great pyramids, to make them strong. So powerful is it that doctors used it in World War I against TB, dysentery and typhus. Onions too are intensely antibacterial and were used as an antiseptic for soldiers' wounds in World War II. There was a well-known tradition of leaving a cut onion in the sickroom to cleanse the atmosphere, because onions absorb bacteria. Vinegar is antiseptic – but it stings. Lavender oil on a cut or burn heals it and prevents scarring.

'Make food your medicine and your medicine your food', said Hippocrates. Oats are soothing to the digestive system.

HONEY

Honey was always included in old herbals and still is a universal cure in folk medicine. From earliest times it was found to be an excellent decongestant, to remove phlegm, and to be antiseptic, and especially healing on burns and lacerations. So highly esteemed was it that Zeus King of the Gods was fed on a diet of milk and honey. Roman soldiers carried honey in their packs for treating wounds. The Ancient Egyptians used it for embalming, since sugar acts as a preservative. Honey was used by the Ancient Greeks to rub the gums in cases of toothache – a remedy still used today by country folk. The vitamin K in honey prevents the acid bacteria which causes decay forming in the mouth. The Koran recommends honey for those who are weak and sick: honey is easily absorbed because it is formed of simple carbohydrates, fructose and glucose, not complex ones which need to be broken down before they are assimilated.

Hayfever and other cures

A neighbour whose bees used to visit my sage and hollyhocks every summer told me that pollen can be used for the treatment of hayfever. Chew honeycomb daily for a month before the hayfever season begins, and the pollen which is present in the wax will immunize the system and work like an inoculation.

Honey is a well-known folk cure for acne: nobody quite knows why, but whatever anti-bacterial properties it contains, the condition is greatly helped by regular applications of honey.

A Scottish medical herbalist told me that if you take 6 teaspoons of honey every 20 minutes, repeated as necessary, your hangover will be no longer. Honey is a good source of potassium, and counteracts the craving which is evidence of potassium deficiency, let alone the craving for sugar. For bruises, apply honey and glycerine in equal parts.

Honey and Cider Vinegar

One of the oldest folk cures in the world for arthritis.

2 teaspoons honey	*2 teaspoons apple cider vinegar*

Mix in a medium-sized mug and fill with hot water. Stir, and drink twice daily.

An old-fashioned bee-skep.

OLD WIVES TALES

A Bahamian grandmother, Elsie, has always used bush medicine to cure family ailments: white sage for measles, the juice of young coconuts for jaundice, okra for an easy birth. Such old wives' tales occur worldwide, sometimes overlapping in cultures that have no contact with each other. They touch on many levels, uniting commonsense and fantasy. They have a wide appeal and mostly can be taken with a large pinch of salt. It is impossible to resist mentioning some non-herbal eccentricities which beg to be included here.

Bee stings: An Aboriginal remedy is to take a small palmful of earth and spit in it. Mix it up into mud and spread over the sting with your finger. Keep moistening it with saliva.

Bone-setting: Third-generation blacksmiths are said to have special powers of healing and especially of setting bones.

Burns: An Italian friend told me to smear a burn with toothpaste – it relieves the pain immediately and heals the skin without a scar.

Colds: From Mineke's childhood in Holland – cut an onion in half, put it cut side up on a saucer by your bedside and your cold goes away.

Corns: A Californian recommends putting a slice of garlic on a corn or wart. Wrap loosely, and it will go in 10 days.

Cramp: Eat honey. Or dip a towel in hot water and apply to the part affected for immediate relief. Several older people have told me to place a wine cork in the pillow slip to prevent night cramps. One said to put your shoes and stockings in the shape of a cross at bedtime, or to place a basin of cold water under the bed, and this will 'draw' the cramp away. A traditional cure in certain parts of the UK is to carry a 'cramp-bone' from a sheep or hare to protect you.

Colic: In Sicily they save a piece of the umbilical cord and rub it over the abdomen of the sick child.

Cuts: A retired farm-worker in East Anglia remembers that when they cut themselves working in the barn they applied a handful of cobwebs to stop the bleeding.

Conjunctivitis: A Scotswoman recommends fresh garden dew rubbed over the eyes.

Epilepsy: Pliny suggested drinking spring water, at night, from the skull of a murdered man.

Goitre: Make a plait from the hair of a stallion's tail and wear around the neck.

Headache: An ancient and long-lasting superstition, from Pliny through to modern European folklore, is to take a rope which has been used to hang a man and tie it around the head. The Irish version suggests doing likewise with the shroud of a recently dead person.

Hangover: Vomit over a frog and then throw it as far away as possible. Or rub a snail or slug into the forehead and do the same.

Insomnia: My Indian friend's mother told her always to eat an onion in the evening meal.

Jaundice: Scandinavian folklore recommends roasting and eating a yellow-hammer. An ancient tale recommends drinking your medicine from a gold goblet.

Lameness: Carry a live shrew in a box around your neck until it dies.

Memory: From Greece – for a bad memory drink sage tea sweetened with honey.

Muscle sprain: From a Chinese woman in Singapore – soak the area in vinegar for a few minutes.

Nosebleed: A woman from Carolina passed down an old wives' tale from her mother: place a drop of vinegar in the ear on the same side as the nosebleed. An English version is to place a cold key down the back of the sufferer. My neighbour suggested nettle juice on lint, up the nostrils.

Pregnancy: A friend who lived in South Africa in the 1940s was told that pawpaw seeds act as a night-after preventive pill.

Paralysis: Carry a live mouse in a box around the neck until it dies: this cures the effects of a stroke.

Rabies: Fry the liver of the mad dog and eat it.

Rheumatism: Several tales come from various sources, including France and Holland. Wear a wash-leather over rheumatic joints, or wear a garter of eel-skin, or carry a stolen potato in your pocket, or wear a copper bracelet, or always carry a chestnut in your pocket.

Stammering: Eat a roasted nightingale.

Sunburn: Rub a cut potato over sunburn for immediate relief, a Brazilian woman told me.

Sore throat: Wrap a red rag around the neck. My neighbour always tied a black stocking around her neck at night and it was gone in the morning.

Toothache: The foot of a mole, cut off while still alive, is worn as an amulet. The eccentric aunt of my Dutch friend, who lived in a quiet farming village near Maastricht, always used to put a rolled up geranium leaf in her ear when she had a bad toothache, and keep it there all day. *Geranium robertianum*, a common wild geranium, has sedative and anti-inflammatory properties.

Dutch wisdom holds that a cut onion by your bed cures a cold.

TRADITIONAL HERBAL REMEDIES

The home medicine-cabinet was an important element of country households worldwide, and still is where transport is slow and communities isolated, far from professional medical help. The ancient wisdom of using herbs to heal everyday disorders was and is practised by the wise man or woman of the community, who pass their knowledge down through the generations. There is usually great wisdom behind the correct use of the right plants: poultices of periwinkle (*Vinca* sp.) were recommended for breast cancer in Suffolk two hundred years ago; now *Vinca* alkaloids from the Madagascan periwinkle *Vinca rosea* are an important medicinal source of anti-leukaemia drugs. Pond scum or algae was used by the Mayans and Aztecs as a medicinal tonic, and now the much-hyped multi-mineral-and-vitamin elixir 'Spirolina', based on this same algae, is a multi-million dollar industry. The North American Indians used chilli peppers to cure and prevent tumours: capsaicin, a substance found in the seeds, is now used to help recovery after chemotherapy. They also used a wild mushroom *Grifola frondosa*, 'hen of the woods', in food and medicine. This is marketed under the name of *maitake* now extensively traded by the Japanese on international markets, and scientists claim that it is the most powerful immune-enhancer in the world and are using it in the treatment of HIV and AIDS.

The world of herbalism is such a vast one that the rigours of selection have forced enormous sins of omission. Only the commonest of plants around the world can be included, and in the briefest synopsis. If you are tempted to make your own traditional cures, be careful: be sure that you pick the correct plant, and that you wash it well before you use it. If in any doubt about the remedy, check with a good herbal encyclopaedia, or ask your local herbalist to advise you on the preparation. Herbs contain powerful substances and must be treated with respect: many have contra-indications and should be used with caution.

Bay (*Laurus nobilis*): Best known for its culinary uses, the stimulating effect of bay can be helpful for a weak digestion, and the oil is antiseptic. Externally it is used as a rub for rheumatism, sprains and bruising.

Left: violet; Below: camomile

Camomile (*Chamaemelum nobile*): Camomile, the 'plant physician', contains muscle relaxants that calm the stomach, soothe sore eyes, and are effective in menstrual disorders. Camomile oil relieves sciatica and arthritis, and can be administered for headaches, migraine and neuralgia.

Coltsfoot (*Tussilago farfara*): The flowers and leaves of coltsfoot have for centuries been smoked to ease a bronchial cough. Pliny recommended this cure as far back as the second century AD, and the Greeks called it 'cough plant'. The leaves were dried, and rolled into home-rolled cigarettes, and are today to be found in herbal tobaccos, although nowadays it is more usual to take coltsfoot in the form of an infusion. It is expectorant and anti-inflammatory and relieves bronchitis, catarrh, asthma, a heavy cough and laryngitis. Although a native of Europe, north and west Asia, and North Africa, coltsfoot (named after the shape of its leaf), has been introduced and naturalized in North America.

Coltsfoot

Comfrey (*Symphytum officinale*): The alternative names of knitbone, boneset and bruisewort aptly describe the uses of comfrey over the centuries. It is however undergoing a lapse in popularity after carcinogenic alkaloids were found to damage liver cells if administered in vast quantities to rats who were given nothing else to eat. It is argued by the opposition that these alkaloids are destroyed on processing the herb and are not absorbed by the human digestive system. Be that as it may, comfrey has a high protein content (35 per cent) and is an important animal food crop in Africa. It contains vitamin B12, unlike any other plant. Above all, comfrey heals damaged tissues: it contains allantoin, a substance which stimulates the production of the connective tissue which forms bone and cartilage. Used for centuries to mend fractures and relieve sprains, comfrey is efficacious on horses too: the leaves wrapped around cracked heels heal them fast. It is a native of Europe and Asia, but grows all over the world.

Dandelion (*Taraxacum officinale*): Dandelion is a powerful diuretic, and dandelion tea (see page 123) is excellent for cellulite, water retention and urinary infections. It detoxifies the system and is beneficial in liver problems and gall bladder infections. You can eat the young leaves in salad and their diuretic action, which eliminates uric acid from the body, is helpful in rheumatism and arthritis. For warts, apply the milky sap from the stem over a few weeks. Originating from central Asia, the dandelion is a very valuable medicinal plant.

Eucalyptus

Dock (*Rumex crispus*): Dock, a native of Eurasia, is now widely distributed in temperate and subtropical countries as a weed. Its long taproot extracts iron from the soil and makes it an excellent remedy for anaemia. Crushed dock leaves are well-known to relieve nettle stings and scalds, and the North American Indians applied them to boils. People have used them on ringworm and scabies, too, with success. Less well known are its detoxifying effects: since the ancient Greeks a decoction of dock has been used to clear up skin complaints and cure digestive problems. The Chinese use it to bring down fever, and dock seeds were a traditional remedy for dysentery and diarrhoea in European folk medicine. Bitter glycosides in the root stimulate the liver and are revitalizing.

Elder (*Sambucus nigra*): The elder has been in long and continuous use ever since the days of Ancient Egypt. Native to Europe, North Africa and western Asia, it was the country medicine chest since all its parts could be used: flowers, leaves, berries, bark and root. The flowers are highly anti-catarrhal, and elderflower tea (see page 123), sometimes mixed with yarrow, is often used in the treatment of colds and flu, or as a gargle for sore throats. The North American Indians used it for colic and also headaches. The berries have a high vitamin C content and are a prophylactic against colds and infections. They have a laxative action and you can add them to other stewed fruits.

This recipe for Elderberry Rob relieves chest troubles, and brings on a sweat to rid the body of toxins.

> *2.25 kg (5lb) ripe elderberries*
> *450g (1lb) sugar*
> *a few cloves*
> *Whisky (optional)*

Simmer the berries and cloves with the sugar until the mixture is the consistency of honey. Strain and bottle. Take 1–2 tablespoons at bedtime in very hot water, adding a tablespoon of whisky if desired.

Eucalyptus (*Eucalyptus globulus*): Indigenous to Australia and Tasmania, infusions of eucalyptus were an Aboriginal remedy for bringing down a fever, for dysentery and sores. A woman who lived in Zimbabwe used a decoction of eucalyptus leaves for colds, coughs and flu, and as a gargle for a sore throat.

Traditional Chinese medicine recommends rubbing diluted eucalyptus oil into inflamed joints to relieve arthritis. It can also be used as a compress for wounds, burns – and athlete's foot! Rub it into the temples when you have a headache, or mix it with tea-tree oil, diluted in a base oil, and rub it into hands and feet as a general tonic to boost the immune system.

Eyebright (*Euphrasia rostkoviana*): Throughout its native Europe, eyebright is still the best known herb to treat eye conditions and has been so since the days of ancient Greece. It sharpens the sight and combats infection. The dried flowering plant is used in infusion and decoction as an anti-inflammatory and astringent, and as a mild lotion it has been used in traditional country medicine to treat conjunctivitis. You can also use this as a nasal douche for catarrh and sinusitis. When applied as a poultice, eyebright aids the healing of minor wounds.

Feverfew (*Tanacetum parthenium*): Today, feverfew is one of the most popular herbs for treating migraine, and is undergoing extensive scientific scrutiny: trials to date report that 70 per cent of migraine sufferers feel an improvement in their condition after taking feverfew. Native to South-East Europe, and introduced

elsewhere around the world, you can easily grow it in the garden with its feathery leaves and daisy-like flowers. Try chewing one or two leaves a day as a prophylactic for headaches and migraines, or make a feverfew sandwich. Do this judiciously: the leaves are very bitter and can cause mouth ulcers or skin irritation.

Lavender (*Lavandula officinalis*): The famous fragrance of lavender is loved for its own sake, but the aromatic oil has powerful remedial values too. It is strongly sedative, so a few drops in a nightime bath will facilitate restful sleep. Some hospitals are now burning lavender oils in their wards instead of administering sleeping pills. Lavender oil is anti-depressant and can be

Lavender

The calming, sedative effect of lavender has been utilised for centuries by country people.

HERBS TO HELP SLEEP

The ancient Greeks recommended drinking wine to make you sleep – obviously in the right dosage! The soporific qualities of the hop are legendary, so beer will have a similar effect. The dried leaves of beautiful lady's mantle, used to fill a pillow, also induce sleep. Country wisdom suggests sleeping on a mattress filled with oat husks, since oats are a well-known nerve tonic. Cider vinegar with honey was recommended on retiring to bed, and medieval folk found that hawthorn tea worked wonders. Principally, however, there are six major herbs that have been used in cures for insomnia for centuries:

Camomile (*Anthemis nobilis* and *Matricaria chamomilla*): Camomile has been a well-established sleep herb since the time of the ancient Egyptians. Indigenous to Europe and northern Asia, it has naturalized in the USA. Culpeper wrote that 'the bathing with a decoction of chamomile taketh away the weariness, and easeth pain'. He recommended the 'flowers boiled in a posset drink' (see page 171). Camomile is a relaxant for the nervous system, soothing, calming and tranquillizing for restless or over-

sensitive people. Its volatile oil with its delicious scent has the effect of relaxing muscles and aiding the digestion.

Chamomile Tea

Make an infusion of 2 tablespoons camomile flower to 600ml (1 pint) boiling water. Stand, covered, for 15 minutes, then strain and sweeten with honey.

Hop (*Humulus lupulus*): Hops grow vigorously in northern temperate zones and are cultivated in Europe, the USA and Chile. Dried hop flowers, the female 'cones' of the hop which are so strongly scented, have been used to make 'hop pillows' for the sleepless for generations. They help to soothe the highly strung, to relax twitching or restless muscles and are a mild sedative. Make a cup of hop tea at bedtime, using the same method as camomile tea (above), for a good restful night's sleep.

Lavender (*Lavandula angustifolia*): This best-loved of aromatics, a native of the Mediterranean but introduced widely elsewhere, can be used to make a pillow in the same way as the hop pillow above, adding if you wish a few hops, some camomile flowers and lime blossoms. Sprinkle a few drops of lavender essential oil over the flowers before you sew up the pillow.

John Parkinson, herbalist and apothecary to King James 1, describes in his *Paradisus in Sole* the fragrance of lavender as 'piercing the senses':

Boil a good handful of lavender flowers in enough water to cover for 10 minutes. Strain into the bath and have a long soak.

Sprinkle a few drops of lavender essential oil or a little good quality lavender water on to your pillow to enhance the effect – and you will be asleep in no time.

Lettuce (*Lactuca virosa*): Lettuce has a very old reputation as a harmless herb to help and encourage sleep. Its country names include sleep-wort. In the eighteenth century lettuces were cultivated for the white sap in the stems which contains lactucanum, used as a sedative up to the end of the nineteenth century. This substance was introduced into medical practice in 1771 and called lettuce opium. It was even used to adulterate true opium, being a mild sedative.

My Chinese friend Frank told me that their 'sleeping milk' or Ku-chin-kan was made from the white juice of the lettuce plant, and that wild lettuce juice was used in other parts of the world too before the days of anaesthetics, to give relief from pain.

So the best advice is to eat a good salad at night to partake of this natural sedative, soothing restlessness and muscle tension. The tale of the Flopsy Bunnies falling asleep after ravaging Mr McGregor's lettuces was based on science!

Lime Flowers (*Tilia cordata*): In ancient times the lime tree was sacred to the Indo-Germanic peoples. The almost overpowering scent of a lime tree in flower comes from the yellowish flowers which bees love and which are used to make the world-famous tisane *tilleul*. Also called linden tea from the old German name for the tree, lind, this mildly honey-scented drink is deliciously soothing to the stomach. It is a nerve tonic, and helps sleeplessness. It is antispasmodic, sedative and diuretic and is used in eastern European folk medicine to reduce blood pressure.

Either make a cup of lime flower tea before retiring to bed, or make an infusion for a soothing bath (see rosemary bath page 92).

Valerian (*Valeriana officinalis*) Valerian has an ancient reputation as a powerful medicinal herb and was promoted by Arab physicians in early times. It still has a place in pharmocopeias worldwide as a non-addictive tranquillizer and has found its way into numerous over-the-counter preparations. It reduces blood pressure, is useful in stress and insomnia, and good for menopausal symptoms. Valerianic acids are found in many sedatives. All-heal, Self-heal and Blessed Herb are among its country names. 'Phu' was another – undoubtedly because of the stink of the crushed roots, which cats love in the same way as they are attracted to catmint, happily rolling in it!

Valerian should only be used on prescription since large doses are inadvisable and it does not mix well with orthodox drugs. But it is powerfully sleep-inducing and soothes the over-sensitive, the tremulous and the irritable, and has been used to effect in nervous exhaustion and anxiety states. Tincture of valerian was used to treat shell shock in World War I.

A small home-made pillow filled with hop flowers induces deep sleep.

HERBAL TEAS AND TISANES

Making infusions of fresh or dried herbs is one of the best methods of extracting their qualities.

Making Herb Teas

Always use good-quality herbs: some packaged dried herbs are almost entirely without aroma or flavour: your nose will tell you.

Using dried herbs

One teaspoon for each cup is the general rule. Put it into a teapot, cover with boiling water, put on the lid and leave to steep for 5–8 minutes. Do not over-brew, as it will ruin the delicacy of the herb. For the most delicately-flavoured herbs, it is better to add more of the herb to the infusion, and brew for a shorter time.

Using fresh herbs

Bruise 3 teaspoons of leaves by crushing them in a clean cloth. Place in the bottom of a small china teapot. Cover with boiling water, put on the lid and leave to infuse.

Using seeds – e.g. fennel, dill, caraway.

Crush them in a clean cloth first, and make the tea with 1 tablespoon per 600ml (1 pint) of water. Put into a saucepan and simmer gently for 5–8 minutes. Strain off, and sweeten with a little honey if desired.

For iced herb teas, make as above, strain, and chill in the refrigerator. These are wonderfully cooling and refreshing in summer. You can serve them with some cold milk and ice for a shake-style drink.

Blackberry leaf (*Rubus fruticosus*): Gather the young leaves in spring. This tea is excellent for skin ulcers and sore throats: it can even be used as a gargle once it has cooled. You can also mix it with other spring leaves – for example, try three parts each of blackberry leaves, wild strawberry leaves and woodruff. Add a pinch of thyme to make a delicious combination which is thirst-quenching and slightly diuretic.

Bergamot (*Monarda didyma*): Red bergamot makes the most fragrant of teas which is soothing and relaxing, excellent taken at bedtime. It has been called Oswego tea, after the Oswego Indians of North America who made it regularly. American colonists took to it when they boycotted British tea in the War of Independence. Bergamot leaves add their inimitable fragrancy to China tea, as well as to wine cups and lemonade.

For a nightcap, pour 300ml (½ pint) milk over 1 tablespoon shredded bergamot leaves and allow to steep for 5 minutes or longer. Sweeten with honey and drink warm.

Camomile (*Chamaemelum nobile* and *Matricaria chamomilla*): This tisane, one of the most famous of them all, is often drunk as a digestive after a meal because it has a soothing action on the gastro-intestinal tract, camomile being sedative and anti-inflammatory. It has

been found to be very good for ageing skin. Sweeten the tisane with honey if desired.

Dandelion (*Taraxacum officinale*) Dandelion tea is strongly diuretic, and improves liver and gall bladder functions, as well as being said to help rheumatism (see page 116). Use fresh leaves. Dandelion is safe in large amounts.

Elderflower (*Sambucus nigra*): An old lady in the village uses elderflower tea for a cold, as an alternative to aspirin. Sometimes her grandmother mixed it with lime flowers to help sweat out a chill or flu, as elderflower's volatile oil promotes sweating. You can also add elderflowers to ordinary tea, to flavour it with a delicate muscatel aroma.

Juniper berry (*Juniperus communis*): Juniper grows from the Mediterraean to the Arctic, in the Himalayas and in North America. Its antiseptic properties are useful in cystitis, it is diuretic and relieves gastric discomfort. It is not to be used in pregnancy or where kidneys are inflamed.

Use about 12–18 berries for each cup, cover with boiling water and leave to steep for 10 minutes. It is palatable sweetened with a little honey if desired.

Lady's Mantle (*Alchemilla vulgaris*): This tea has been used throughout Europe, its native habitat, for gynaecological disorders. 'Woman's best friend' it has been called by country people, as its

regular use relieves menstrual pain and excessive bleeding. It is astringent and anti-inflammatory and is highly recommended for the menopause.

Lemon balm (*Melissa officinalis*) I make this tea in early summer with a large bunch of the young leaves, infusing them in hot water for 10 minutes, and drinking it in the sun. It is sensational: light, refreshing and aromatic. The ancient Greeks called it a cure-all: it is sedative and a gentle herb for upset stomachs. It has long been used for depression or over-tiredness, and for anxiety and tension headaches.

Peppermint (*Mentha* spp.) Made with fresh peppermint leaves, this tea is one of the most attractive of them all. Its anti-spasmodic properties calm the stomach, and it is good for nervous headaches, as well as for colds. Use whole leaves for a more subtle flavour, or shred them if you want to make it stronger. A delicious drink can be made by infusing a tablespoon of peppermint leaves in 300ml (½ pint) boiling milk for 7–10 minutes, then straining off. Serve hot.

Similar teas can be made with rose geranium (*Pelargonium graveolens*), rosehip (*Rosa canina*), sage (*Salvia officinalis*), thyme (*Thymus vulgaris*), and lemon verbena (*Aloysia triphylla*). You can also make delightful combination teas such as balm with lavender, hawthorn with sage, sage with honeysuckle and yarrow with elderflower.

HERBAL LORE AND LEGEND

The lore and legends of herbs have filled many books from antique times, but certain anecdotes and associations have found their way into popular culture via long-standing traditions, or been made famous by literature and poetry.

Balm (*Melissa officinalis*): Balm is the 'scholars' herb, given to students to clear their heads and sharpen both their memory and their understanding. In the Language of Flowers, balm stands for joking because it makes people cheerful and merry, and composes even the most agitated. It has a 'cordial and exhilarating effect', according to John Evelyn, the seventeenth-century diarist, and wearing a sachet of balm leaves next to your heart will make you attractive, happy and healthy. The farmer's wife would give balm leaves to her cows to increase the flow of milk, and balm is 'good against a surfeit of mushrooms.'

Basil (*Ocimum basilicum*): Every good Hindu goes to his final rest with a basil leaf on his breast – his passport to Paradise. The Hindus believe that good fortune awaits those who build their houses on a spot where basil has grown freely, and there is no forgiveness in this world or the next for anyone who uproots it.

In Italy the leaves of basil are love tokens, and a pot of basil in the window is a sign that a girl is expecting her lover, while in Crete, basil is sown in pots as a love plant. In France, however, *semer le basilic* means to slander someone. To dream of basil means grief and misfortune.

Dill (*Anethum graveolens*): Dill is a powerful herb in the armoury of witches who used it in their spells and charms. Yet it was also powerful against witches, hung over doors or windows as a protection against the Evil Eye. It is generally a plant of good omen: English country brides used to wear a sprig of dill on their wedding day.

Fennel (*Foeniculum vulgare*): Prometheus concealed the fire of the sun in a hollow stalk of fennel to bring it from heaven to earth for the human race, according to ancient Greek legend. Knowledge came to man from the gods of Olympus in the form of a fiery coal contained in a fennel stalk. It is a powerfully protective plant against witchcraft, and sprigs of fennel hung in the rafters would drive evil spirits away. In classical times fennel was strewn across the pathway of a newly-married couple.

Lavender (*Lavandula vera/angustifolia*): Lavender is dedicated to Hecate, the goddess of the moon revered by witches and sorcerers. Yet ambiguously it was one of the herbs used to avert the Evil Eye. In the Language of Flowers, lavender represents 'mistrust' and it was believed that the viper made lavender its habitat. Legend goes that lions and tigers become docile with the scent of lavender.

Rosemary (*Rosmarinus officinalis*): Rosemary has more folklore attached to it than any other herb. The blue flowers are said to have taken their colour from the Virgin Mary's blue cloak when, during the flight into Egypt, she threw it over a rosemary bush to dry: up until then the flowers had been white. Rosemary grows to the height of Christ and no higher, and for no longer than his 33 years of age. Rosemary grows in the gardens of the righteous, and where it grows 'mistress is master'. At country weddings sprigs of rosemary were dipped into the wine before the newlyweds drank, to ensure their continued love and happiness. Rosemary stands for remembrance.

Sage (*Salvia officinalis*): 'Sage the Saviour' was believed to prolong life:

> *He that would live for aye*
> *Must eat sage in May*

A thriving sage bush indicates thriving family fortunes and it flourishes or withers according to the prosperity of the master of the house. But

> *If the sage tree thrives and grows*
> *The master's not master and he knows!*

In the Language of Flowers it stands for esteem, and sage plants were valued so highly that they needed protection from the Devils' familiar, the toad. So rue was often planted nearby in order to attract them away from this valuable plant.

Salvia officinalis

Anethum graveolens

Lavandula stoechas

THE COUNTRY
HARVEST

The celebration of plenty happens all over the world, and in many forms. The rice harvest in Japan is celebrated with traditional festivities dedicated to Inari the rice goddess. In India, Vishnu and Lakshmi are offered a dish of rice or idli (steamed rice cakes), or newly harvest grains cooked with cashew nuts and jaggery (raw lump cane sugar). The olive harvest is marked in the South of France at Nyons with the pageantry of Les Olivades where the Knights of the Olive Trees parade through the town, and 'pan bagna' – bread soaked in olive oil – is eaten. In parts of the world where fish is plentiful the fish harvest is celebrated: on the Volga in Southern Russia Maslenitsa in mid-June celebrates their 'living silver', the catch of bream and sturgeon. At Taranto in Italy in September a feast is dedicated to Stella Maris – Star of the Sea – who protects fishermen at sea, and special fish barbecues are set up along the beaches. In New Mexico an annual chilli festival is held to celebrate the country's biggest cash crop, and California celebrates its 'silver pearl' in a famous event at Gilroy where thousands turn out to pay homage to garlic. There are Chestnut Fairs in southern France around All Souls Day, November 1st, and honey fairs the world over. The mushroom harvest in Russia is a national pastime, immortalized by Tolstoy, and at the annual Apple Tree festival in Finistère, Brittany, a grand fair and firework display marks the celebrations amid much cider-making.

Before the mechanization of farming, the end of the grain harvest with its 'Harvest Home' feast was the crowning point of the farm worker's year, celebrating the filling of the granaries with the year's crop. Wilf my neighbour in the village told me how the Last Sheaf was brought home in triumph, the harvest wain decorated with flowers and boughs of oak and ash. It was drawn by four or six great working horses, decked out with garlands of wild flowers. That evening a harvest supper – the 'Horkey' – was held at the big barn for all the farm workers, a traditional roast meat meal followed by apple pie and plum pudding, and washed down with generous amounts of ale or cider. They danced and sang and toasted the farmer and his family. An American lad who worked on his father's farm in South Dakota remembers the obligatory church service before a similar harvest supper, with a rousing sermon to send them on their way. The Harvest Festival service held in many churches is a remnant of this custom.

This wild harvest can be converted into preserves of many kinds – pickles, chutneys, jams and jellies, and even unusual marmalades to stock the larder for the winter months. The annual mushroom feast provides you not only with the delights of gathering them from the damp woods, but also with many delicious meals while they are in season, and the honey harvest from your local beekeeper may well furnish your kitchen shelf with enough to make some delectable sweet treats. Pies and soufflés, cakes and puddings, cookies and ice-creams can all find their way to the table from the hedgerows, fields and woods.

Grandmother's Dairy

Fresh eggs and new milk were part and parcel of the meals in Hallington Hall, the summer home of the distinguished historian G. M. Trevelyan, where as children we spent regular holidays. Still warm from the adjoining farm they were brought solemnly to table in the formal dining-room in elegant china jugs or silver dishes. The fruit used to come from the great walled kitchen garden with its long greenhouses, espaliered trees and huge fruit cages, collected daily for the kitchens by Sidney the gardener. My mother got on well with the cook, Mrs Thomas, and I remember her jotting down recipe tips. After she died I found these written up into a little exercise book, and some of the dairy and egg recipes here come from that source. The cook made delicious country pies and puddings too, which I have never seen anywhere else.

Lemon creams.

Lemon Creams

This is pure bliss. Cool and delicious for hot summer days, you can make it with wine instead of sherry for a lighter effect. Eat with soup spoons – it's like a sweet soup.

SERVES 6	
600ml (1 pint) crème fraîche	3–4 tablespoons caster sugar, to taste
50g (2oz) ground almonds	Lemon rind, to decorate
3 glasses sherry	2 tablespoons golden syrup, to
Rind and juice of 1 lemon	decorate

Mix the crème fraîche with the ground almonds and pour into a jug. In another jug put the sherry, lemon rind and juice, and sugar to taste. Pour rapidly from one jug to the other until the mixture is frothy, then pour into wine glasses. Chill. To decorate, heat the golden syrup with the decorative lemon rind for 1–2 minutes, then pour on top of the individual servings.

Baked Apple Custard

Apples are a symbol of fruitfulness and plenty, and friends in Normandy say always to leave the last apple on the tree for good luck. This apple dessert is a lovely, unusual pudding which ends up with a marbled effect as the apple and the custard separate. Serve chilled, with thin cream.

SERVES 4	
6 large apples, peeled and cored	300ml (½ pint) milk
A little cold water	4 eggs
Soft brown sugar, to taste	100g (4oz) caster sugar
Grated rind of half a lemon	1 small cox's apple
1 teaspoon ground cinnamon	25g (1oz) butter

Preheat the oven to 180°C/350°F/gas 4. Heat the apples in a pan with the water and as they begin to soften, mash them to a pulp. Sweeten with brown sugar, add the lemon rind and cinnamon and leave to cool. (A tip to soften hardened brown sugar: add a slice of bread or apple to the container and leave for a couple of days.) Put the apple purée into the bottom of a pie dish. Heat the milk to just below boiling point. Beat the eggs with the sugar until thick, then gradually pour on the hot milk. Pour this over the apple purée, place the dish in the oven and bake for 25–35 minutes. Decorate with pan-fried slices of cox's apple cooked in butter.

Elderflower Floating Islands

I have always loved the muscatel scent of elderflowers, and use them often in jams and soft drinks. I have based this on a classic recipe from France, *Iles flottantes*.

SERVES 4

2 clusters elderflowers	*100g (4oz) caster sugar*
1.2 litres (2 pints) milk	*Pinch of salt*
2 tablespoons semolina	*4 eggs, separated*
	Ground cinnamon

Snip the blossoms off the stalks and infuse them in the milk over a low heat for 10 minutes. (An old-fashioned tip to prevent milk from boiling over is to place a clean marble in the bottom of the pan.) Strain the milk and stir in the semolina, half of the sugar and the salt. Beat the egg yolks in a bowl, then pour over the milk and semolina mixture. Set the bowl over hot (not boiling) water, and heat gently, stirring until the custard thickens. Pour into a glass dish to cool.

Just before serving, beat the egg whites until stiff, add the remaining sugar and beat again until the mixture resembles uncooked meringue. Scoop up tablespoons of the meringue and float on top of the custard. Decorate with a sprinkling of cinnamon.

Hazelnut Ice-cream

Hazelnuts, cobnuts, filberts, call them what you will, are all names for the same wild nut, dedicated to St Phillibert whose saint's day falls at the end of August, at about the time of the hazelnut harvest. Their crunchiness contrasts with the smooth creaminess of the ice-cream and is mouthwatering.

SERVES 6

100g (4oz) hazelnuts, ground	*12g (½oz) butter*
in a blender	*75g (3oz) caster sugar*
600ml (1 pint) milk	*4 eggs, separated*

Simmer the nuts with the milk in a heavy pan for 20 minutes. Put the butter, sugar and egg yolks into a bowl, set over hot – not boiling – water and beat together. Gradually add the milk and nuts

Baked apple custard.

to the mixture, beating until thick. Do not let it reach boiling point or it will separate. Pour into a container and when cool put into the freezer. Freeze for 1 hour until well-chilled. Beat the egg whites stiffly and fold into the ice-cream. Return to the freezer.

English Custard

As children we used to beg our Northumbrian cook Mrs Thomas to make this for us most nights. Sometimes she made it with duck eggs for richness, and occasionally she even used cream for a superlatively rich custard.

SERVES 8

600ml (1 pint) milk	*Rind of half a lemon*
75g (3oz) granulated sugar	*A few drops vanilla essence*
	5 eggs

Put the milk into a pan with the sugar, lemon rind and vanilla, and leave to infuse over a low heat for 30 minutes. Bring to boiling point, then strain into a bowl. Beat the eggs and stir into the cooling milk. Strain into a bowl and set it over a pan of hot water. Stir until the mixture thickens. Do not allow it to reach boiling point otherwise it will curdle. Serve with pies and other desserts.

EGGS

Some of my earliest memories of childhood are of my mother rounding up the chickens into the hen house every evening, and of one inevitably escaping and causing havoc in a neighbour's garden. The flavour of those eggs, and the rich colour of the yolks, was sensational. There was also, unknown to me, a rich and varied harvest out there somewhere of gulls' eggs, goose eggs, the eggs of plovers, moorhens, ostriches, partridges, pheasants, pigeons, quail, turkeys and guinea fowl. Even penguins. Eggs for the specialists.

Hens' eggs, however, are both eaten and celebrated the world over, from China with its thousand-year-old eggs (preserved in salt, wood-ash and lime), to a tiny village in the French Alps where the reappearance of the sun from behind the mountains after one hundred days of deepest winter is celebrated with a cook-in of omelettes. The obvious symbolism of eggs as life-force, of the unending cycle of creativity, ensures their place in Easter festivities throughout the Christian world – boiled, painted, blown, or imitated in chocolate.

Apple Snow

My mother used to make this for the family and we all loved it. I still use her recipe, which she had inherited from Mrs Thomas in her Northumberland kitchen.

SERVES 4	
5 large apples, peeled, cored and cut into quarters	Finely grated rind of half a lemon
	4 egg whites
	100g (4oz) caster sugar

Put the apples into a pan with the lemon rind and a little water, just to prevent burning. Cook until tender, about 20 minutes, then mash them to a pulp and leave to cool.

Whisk the egg whites, add the sugar, and continue whisking until the mixture is stiff. Gently fold into the apples, and heap in a large glass dish. This is lovely with a dish of custard (see page 131).

Elderflower Fritters

For me, midsummer means elderflowers. I use this plentiful harvest to flavour gooseberry jams and pies, and every year I make my own elderflower cordial. These fritters are exceptionally delicious, served simply with a sprinkling of fine sugar and a touch of powdered cinnamon.

SERVES 4	Batter:
8 stalks of elderflowers, flowerheads snipped off	100g (4oz) plain flour
Caster sugar and a little cinnamon	A pinch of salt
	3 tablespoons vegetable oil
Vegetable oil for deep-frying	150ml (¼ pint) warm water
	1 egg white, stiffly beaten

To make the batter, sift the flour with the salt, and stir in the oil. Gradually add the water, stirring until smooth and creamy. Leave to stand for 2 hours. Just before using, fold in the beaten egg white.

Dip the flowerheads in the prepared batter and deep-fry in very hot oil for about 1 minute until golden and crisp. Drain on kitchen paper, dust with caster sugar and cinnamon and serve immediately.

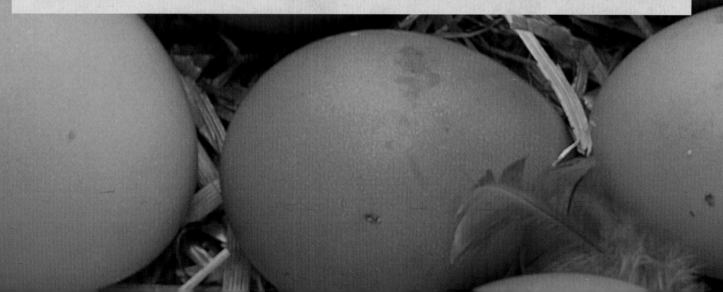

Hazelnut and White Chocolate Meringue

Hazelnuts grow thickly in the hedges near a village in northern France where a friend lets out her cottage. Inspired by a meal at the local restaurant I tried my hand at this blissful dessert, light and nutty yet with a hint of chocolate. Sandwich it with whipped cream and it is fit for a special occasion.

SERVES 6–8

100g (4oz) hazelnuts

5 egg whites

225g (8oz) caster sugar

75g (3oz) each plain and white chocolate, chopped roughly

1 teaspoon cinnamon or ground mixed spice

300ml (½ pint) double cream

Icing sugar, for dusting

A few raspberries (optional)

Line two large baking sheets with baking parchment. Preheat the oven to 140°C/275°F/gas 1.

Toast the nuts and chop them finely. Beat the egg whites until stiff, then beat in the sugar until stiff and shiny. Fold in the nuts and the chocolate. Spoon the mixture into two large rounds on the prepared baking sheets and bake for 2–2½ hours. Turn off the oven and leave there to cool.

Whip the cream until fairly thick, and spread it over the top of one of the rounds. Cover with the second, dust with icing sugar, decorate with a few raspberries if desired and it is ready to serve.

A tip for using up eggshells: add to cloudy stock to clear it, and remove afterwards (they absorb impurities).

Pickled red cabbage.

PICKLES

The pungent smell of pickles cooking with vinegar is highly evocative of autumn, reminiscent of those first chilly misty mornings as summer fades and you feel a warning of winter in the fields and lanes. You can make a huge variety of pickles, some exotic, others traditional: the range extends from cauliflower, shallot, artichoke and beetroot to melon, peach and pear, as well as to many oriental vegetables.

When you are making pickles, do use good vinegar: it is a false economy to buy it cheaply because nasty vinegar will affect the entire flavour of whatever you are cooking. Check that it has an acetic content of at least 5 per cent and use white vinegar because it shows off the colour of the pickle better than dark vinegar. Store your pickles in glass jars with plastic screw tops – metal lids will corrode on storage.

The Russians have a time-honoured tradition of pickling mushrooms, and the Chinese pickle a variety of vegetables for winter use. Szechuan preserved vegetables are pickled in salt and chilli and eaten as they are, or added to stir-fries. The pickled vegetables or delicate *tsukemono* of Japanese cuisine have a crisp texture and tangy flavour and are often eaten with rice as a lunchtime snack. They are traditionally pressed and pickled in rice bran and salt.

Spiced Pickling Vinegar

900 ml (1½ pints) vinegar
12 g (½ oz) each whole cloves, allspice berries, root ginger, cinnamon sticks, whole peppercorns

Warm the vinegar in an aluminium preserving pan. Add the spices, cover and infuse over a low heat for 2 hours. Leave to cool. When cool, strain the vinegar into clean bottles and seal.

Pickled Red Cabbage

A great stand-by for the larder shelf, this particular recipe comes from Ireland.

MAKES 4 X 600ML (I PINT) JARS
1 medium red cabbage
4 tablespoons salt
900ml (1½ pints) spiced pickling vinegar (see above)

Remove the outer cabbage leaves and divide the rest into 6 segments. Remove the core, and shred the leaves very finely. Put the cabbage into a large bowl and sprinkle with salt. Cover and leave in a cold place for 1–2 days.

Drain the cabbage but do not rinse. Pack into clean jars and top up with spiced vinegar. Seal, and store in a cool dry place for at least 3 weeks before using. Eat within 3 months, otherwise the cabbage loses its crispness.

Old-fashioned Gooseberry Vinegar

This vinegar is at its best if you leave it to mature for a year, when it makes the most superb vinaigrette and is a deliciously different change from the more usual raspberry vinegar. You can use as many gooseberries as you wish, as long as you use the right proportion of water and sugar. I tend to use about 1.35kg (3lb) fruit and enough water to cover.

Ripe gooseberries, topped and tailed
Lukewarm water
Brown sugar

Process the gooseberries in a blender until they are roughly mashed, but not puréed. Place in a bowl with enough lukewarm water to cover, and leave to soak for 24 hours. Strain through a sieve and measure the liquid. For every 600ml (1 pint) add 150g (5oz) sugar. Stir well, then pour into a large cask and cover. Stir 2–3 times a day until the sugar dissolves completely, then secure a linen cloth over the bunghole. Leave to stand for 9 months in a warm place in the kitchen, then decant into bottles. Store for at least 12 months before using.

Pickled Blackberries

These are an inspired addition to the larder shelf, delicious with bread and cheese. I also love them with cream cheese and fine sugar as a dessert. Beware however of picking blackberries after October 12th. The legend goes that this is the anniversary of the Fall, and that Satan, cast out of heaven, fell into a blackberry bush and cursed it in his anger. From that date on blackberries taste sour, so they say.

MAKES 1.8 KG (4LB)

450g (1lb) preserving sugar
300ml (½ pint) white wine
  vinegar
1 teaspoon allspice berries
1 teaspoon cloves
2 x 7cm (3in) cinnamon sticks
900g (2lb) blackberries

Put the sugar into a pan with the vinegar and dissolve slowly over a low heat. Tie the spices in a muslin bag and place in the simmering mixture for 5 minutes. Add the blackberries and simmer gently for a further 10–15 minutes. Remove the spices and strain the blackberries through a nylon sieve reserving the liquid. Pack the berries into warm jars to about two-thirds full. Return the liquid to the pan and boil hard until it reduces to a thick syrup. Pour the syrup over the blackberries to fill the jars, and seal.

Pickled blackberries can be eaten at teatime, and are also delicious with a 'ploughman's lunch'.

Indian chutney (see page 139).

CHUTNEYS

In traditional country cooking, chutneys are made principally from apples, onions and tomatoes, with dried fruits such as sultanas, raisins and dates added. Garlic and shallots can be added, and frequently chutneys are laced with chillies, peppercorns or mustard seed to give a zing. The word chutney actually originates from the Hindi *chatni*, meaning a relish of sweet fruits or vegetables cooked with vinegar and hot spices. Some Indian chutneys however are made up uncooked and served alongside the meal rather like condiments.

Chutneys have always been served with the famous ploughman's lunch: bread and cheese and chutney is one of the best of simple meals when all the ingredients are top quality. They are delicious with curries, with rice dishes, and make a pleasant change to go with roast chicken. A selection of chutneys greatly enhances a buffet table, adding character and flavour to salads and cold dishes.

A practical tip: don't use metal screw-top lids because the vinegar corrodes them.

Old-fashioned tomato and apple chutney

Plain country bread, cheese and pickles was the traditional 'packed lunch' for farm workers to sustain their energy as they worked outside in the fields. Now famous as a 'ploughman's lunch', this can be a wonderful meal if you use quality cheeses, fresh bread and, of course, your own home-made chutneys.

Old-Fashioned Tomato and Apple Chutney

If you grow your own tomatoes you may, in a good year, be overwhelmed by your harvest. So use up either ripe or green tomatoes in this chutney – an admirable way of dealing with a late summer glut.

MAKES 5.4KG (12LB)

2.7kg (6lb) tomatoes, sliced
450g (1lb) apples, cored
450g (1lb) onions, peeled
50g (2oz) coriander seeds
12g (½oz) dried chillies
1½ tablespoons salt
25g (1oz) ground ginger
450g (1lb) demerara sugar
450g (1lb) sultanas
Juice of 1 lemon
4 tablespoons golden syrup
750ml (1¼ pints) malt
    vinegar

Place the sliced tomatoes, apples and onions in a preserving pan. Tie the coriander seeds and chillies in a muslin bag and add to the pan. Sprinkle with the salt and leave overnight. Add the remaining ingredients the next day and bring everything to the boil. Increase the heat to medium and boil for 2 hours until thick. Pack into warm, clean jars before covering and storing.

Indian Chutney

From chutney's country of origin and given to me by an excellent Indian cook, this is not for timid taste-buds.

MAKES 3.5 KG (8LB)	
15 large cooking apples	225g (8oz) raisins
225g (8oz) onions, chopped	450g (1lb) demerara sugar
100g (4oz) garlic, chopped	1.8 litres (3 pints) malt vinegar
2 fresh chillies, sliced	50g (2oz) mustard seeds
	50g (2oz) ground ginger

Bake the apples at 180°C/350°F/gas 4 for 25–30 minutes, until soft. Scoop out the flesh from the skins and remove the pips.

Meanwhile, put the chopped onion into a pan with the garlic and cover with water. Simmer for 20 minutes until soft, then drain. Discard the cooking liquid.

Put the apples and onions into a preserving pan with the remaining ingredients. Bring to the boil and simmer for 20–30 minutes until well amalgamated and most of the liquid has evaporated.

Pack into warm clean jars and leave to cool, then cover and seal.

Autumn Chutney

I first came across this on an annual fund-raising market stall in the village hall, made by a woman who has become a great recipe-swopping friend. This chutney makes the most of the autumn harvest and is wonderful to have on the larder shelf through the winter.

MAKES 3.2 KG/7 LB	
450g (1lb) plums, halved and stoned	450g (1lb) sultanas
450g (1lb) apples, peeled and cored	600ml (1 pint) malt vinegar
450g (1lb) tomatoes, chopped	¼ teaspoon mace
450g (1lb) onions, sliced	¼ teaspoon ground mixed spice
1 large garlic clove, chopped	12g (½ oz) ground ginger
	450g (1lb) demerara sugar

Mix the fruit and vegetables together and put into a preserving pan with all the other ingredients except the sugar. Simmer for 30–40 minutes until tender. Add the sugar and stir until dissolved. Simmer gently, stirring frequently until thick. Cool, then pack into clean jars. Cover with waxed discs, seal and store in a cool, dark, dry place.

Smooth Gooseberry Chutney

One of my greatest favourites: this is almost like a purée in texture, full of interesting flavours, and excellent served with hot or cold meats. It is lovely with cheese, too, and does a lot to spice up a simple side salad.

450g (1lb) gooseberries	450g (1lb) soft brown sugar
225g (8oz) onions, peeled and chopped	15g (½oz) salt
	1 tablespoon ground ginger
300ml (½ pint) chilli or herb vinegar (available from most supermarkets)	½ teaspoon cayenne
	300ml (½ pint) vinegar
	300ml (½ pint) water

Poach the gooseberries in water to cover for 5 minutes, and then drain. Liquidize with the chopped onions and spiced vinegar. Add the remaining ingredients and bring to the boil. Simmer for 15–20 minutes until it is the consistency of a thick sauce. Cool and pack into warm, sterilized jars.

Wild Damson Chutney

There is a damson tree along one of the lanes near to my cottage and when it fruits abundantly I make jellies and jams and cheeses – and this inimitable chutney. The best thing ever with a ploughman's lunch.

MAKES 1.25KG (2 ½LB)	
450g (1lb) wild damsons, stems removed	450ml (¾ pint) malt vinegar
	7g (¼oz) each cloves and root ginger
1 large cooking apple, peeled, cored and chopped	Half a dried red chilli
	1 teaspoon salt
1 large onion, chopped	Pinch of dry mustard powder
75g (3oz) sultanas	350g (12oz) sugar

Cook the damsons gently in a little water until soft, but not breaking up. Drain. Remove the stones with a slotted spoon. Put the fruit into a preserving pan with all the other ingredients except the sugar, tying up the spices in a muslin bag. Simmer gently for 20–30 minutes. Add the sugar and boil hard until thick, stirring from time to time to prevent the mixture sticking to the bottom of the pan. Cool a little, then pour into clean jars. Cover with waxed discs, and seal.

JAMS AND JELLIES

Making jams and jellies was a matter of course for our grandmothers. These women were highly creative, making preserves using whatever grew around them and often in inspired and unusual combinations of ingredients. I have collected numerous old recipe books, and over the have years shared many recipes with other village cooks. The country markets are a great source not only of ideas but also of quality products, and this informal research has furnished me with a fabulous selection of gleaming jars for the larder shelf as well as hundreds of useful tips – not least among my favourites is that of adding chopped nuts to jam.

Making jams is synonymous with homeliness, and much traditional wisdom has accrued from it over the years: always pick your fruit on a dry day to reduce the chances of preserves going mouldy; always use ripe or just under-ripe, and never damaged, fruit, for similar reasons. Use lump, preserving or granulated sugar (in that order of preference). You will need a large, heavy-bottomed preserving pan so that the jam can boil rapidly without boiling over, a long-handled wooden spoon, a slotted spoon, and a jam thermometer (see right). Always store preserves in a cool, dark, dry place to minimize the chances of mould.

It is best to gather fruits in dry weather, in the morning with the sun on them if possible, when their flavour is fullest. Damp weather dilutes the flavour and encourages mould at a later stage. For jams the general rule is to discard over-ripe or unripe fruit, and use as soon as possible after gathering it. For jellies and chutneys you can use damaged and windfall fruit, so long as it is under-ripe and the damaged parts are cut away. In this way you can make full use of food from the garden as well as from the wild – plums or damsons, blackberries or quince, apples or crab-apples – all the fruits that have long played their part in the rich harvest of the autumn countryside.

Testing for a Set

Making jams and jellies is an incredibly simple operation, but the crucial part comes when setting point is reached. Some jams take longer than others to set, depending on the water content of the fruit. The time taken can vary from under ten minutes to over twenty. It is when the mixture becomes thick and syrupy that it is approaching setting point. You need to have an infallible method of testing for it. The 'saucer test' is one: as the jelly or jam begins to thicken, put a teaspoon of the mixture on to a cold saucer and let it cool for a few minutes. If the jam or jelly wrinkles a little and does not run when you tilt the saucer, or move it with your fingertip, it is ready. If it is still liquid, continue boiling and repeat a little later. Alternatively, use a jam thermometer which will have a setting point marked on it. The only piece of special equipment you need for jelly is either a jelly bag or a large piece of muslin to strain the liquid.

Pumpkin Preserve

I have been making this highly unusual jam for years. It is excellent on toast for breakfast, and I also use it as a filling for sponge cakes. It looks stunning: it ends up a pale gold colour, clear and translucent, with a mouthwatering texture to it. Personally I love the spike of the ginger!

MAKES 4.5KG (10LB)	
2.7kg (6lb) pumpkin, peeled, deseeded and cut into small cubes	600ml (1 pint) lemon juice
	600ml (1 pint) water
2.7kg (6lb) sugar	About 100g (4oz) crystallized stem ginger, to taste (optional)

Layer the pumpkin in a deep dish with the sugar. Pour the lemon juice over the top and leave overnight. Place the pumpkin in a preserving pan with the water and cook until tender, about 30–40 minutes. Leave to stand overnight. Drain off the syrup, boil it up until it is quite thick, and skim. Pour the boiling syrup over the pumpkin. Add the ginger, cut into small cubes, if using. Spoon into jars and seal.

Old-fashioned Gooseberry Jam

A lovely summer jam from an old lady in the village. It is delicious on scones. This recipe uses currant juice instead of water to cook the fruit: you can reduce any scum on top by stirring in a lump of butter just as the jam begins to set, or rub the inside of the pan

Golden pumpkin preserve, spiked with ginger.

with butter before you start. A further precaution is to add 2 tablespoons of vinegar to the water in which you sterilize the jars.

MAKES 2.7KG (6LB)

450g (1lb) redcurrants or
blackcurrants
600ml (1 pint) water

2.7kg (6lb) red gooseberries,
topped and tailed
1.4kg (3lb) sugar

Put the currants into a pan with the water and simmer for 10 minutes. Leave to cool, then strain off the juice.

Place the gooseberries in a preserving pan with 600ml (1 pint) of the currant juice. Bring to the boil and simmer fast until the gooseberries begin to break up. Add the sugar and simmer slowly until setting point is reached (see opposite). Pot in warm jars, and seal.

Lemon and Rhubarb Jam

A useful rule of thumb is never to fill your preserving pan more than halfway, since jams are liable to boil over and make a terrible sticky mess on the stove. This is a stunning jam for early summer, with the slight crunchiness of a few chopped almonds. Delectable.

MAKES 1.4KG (3LB)

1.4kg (3lb) rhubarb, cut into
chunks
900g (2lb) sugar

Finely grated rind of 2 lemons
25g (1oz) almonds, skinned
and chopped very finely

Put the rhubarb into a pan with the sugar. Boil very gently, stirring constantly, for 30 minutes. Add the lemon rind and chopped almonds, and boil to setting point. Pot in warm jars, and seal

Great-Grandmother's Strawberry Jam

The secret of success with strawberry jam is not to cook it too long, and not to use too much sugar, otherwise the delicate flavour of this exquisite summer fruit is impaired. If by any chance your jam does not set (you can use this tip for other jams too) try adding 1–2 teaspoons of fresh lemon juice to every 450g (1lb) fruit, and bringing to setting point again. The pectin in the lemon should do the trick.

MAKES 2.4KG (5LB)

1.8kg (4lb) strawberries

1.4kg (3lb) sugar

Choose a sunny day to gather the strawberries for this jam and leave them in the sun until ready to use: this treatment preserves the colour perfectly. Use as fresh fruit as possible, and wash it carefully, being careful not to bruise the berries. Remove the stalks and discard any bruised or damaged fruit before use.

Put the strawberries and sugar into a pan and cook briskly for 15–20 minutes. Then remove the strawberries and spread them out in flat dishes in the sun. Boil the syrup until it is thick and clear, then return the strawberries to the pan. Pot in warm jars and seal.

Making jellies in autumn is the perfect way of preserving the wild fruit harvest for the year ahead.

Pear, Orange and Walnut Jam

The best jam in the world. The recipe was given to me years ago by a woman who lived in a village in the depths of Burgundy, and I have made it over and over again. I shall never forget how it first tasted on baguettes from the boulangerie for breakfast, with a pot of fresh coffee.

MAKES 2.2KG (5LB)	1.4 kg (3lb) sugar
2 oranges, peeled and finely chopped	450g (1lb) sultanas or raisins
1.4kg (3lb) pears, peeled, cored and finely sliced	300ml (½ pint) water
	175g (6oz) walnuts, chopped roughly

Place the fruit in a preserving pan with the sugar, sultanas and water, and simmer for 1½ hours. Add the chopped walnuts and cook for a further 15 minutes. Pot and seal.

Plum Jelly

I make this superb jelly with my neighbour's Victoria plums when she has a glut that she cannot cope with: it is a memorable tea-time treat on scones. One of the problems with jelly-making is losing the wooden spoon in the pan, however long its handle. An American lady gave me this tip: clip a wooden peg to the handle of the spoon and it will lodge securely on the edge of the pan.

MAKES 3.6KG (8LB)	Juice of 1 lemon
2.7kg (6lb) plums, stems removed	Water and sugar

Slit the plums and put into a preserving pan with the lemon juice and enough water to cover. Simmer gently until the fruit is tender, about 30 minutes. Place a jelly bag over a large bowl and tip the contents into it (or alternatively pour through muslin and tie up over the bowl). Allow to drip for an hour or two. Do not squeeze the bag because this will strain impurities into the jelly and make it cloudy.

Measure the strained juice and for every 600ml (1 pint) allow 400g (14oz) sugar. Return the juice to the clean preserving pan, bring to the boil, then remove from the heat and stir in the sugar. Dissolve it over a low heat and then simmer until setting point is reached (see page 140).

Remove the pan from the heat, skim off any scum and pour the jelly into warm clean jars. Cool then cover with waxed paper and seal.

Japonica Jelly

I have a japonica tree trained to the front of my cottage and it rewards me with exquisitely elegant salmon-pink blossoms in the spring, and a surprisingly abundant harvest of yellow fruits in October. So there is an annual ritual of japonica-jelly-making for our winter breakfasts: inimitable on toast, and a weekend treat with croissants. It is the most heavenly dark pink, and not unlike quince jelly.

japonica fruit	sugar
water	

Wash the fruit and discard any over-ripe or damaged ones. Cut in half, or into quarters if they are large. Put into a preserving pan with water to cover and simmer until tender – about 45 minutes. Strain off the juice by pouring into a jelly bag, or large sheet of muslin, over a large bowl. Hang the bag over the bowl to drip until dry – anything from 2 hours to overnight. Do not squeeze the bag otherwise impurities in the fruit will cause the jelly to go cloudy.

Measure the juice into the clean preserving pan. For every 600ml (1 pint) juice add 350g (12oz) sugar. Allow it to dissolve over a gentle heat, then bring to the boil and simmer to setting point (see page 140). Pour into warm, clean jars, cover with waxed paper and seal. Store in a cool dark place.

An alternative to carrot marmalade can also be made with a 50:50 mixture of rhubarb and carrots.

MARMALADES

Although 'marmalade' nowadays means a jam made from citrus fruits, its origin lies in conserves of other fruit, usually quince. *Marmelo* is the Portuguese for quince, and in early days a thick quince paste not unlike the cotignac (right) was a common sweetmeat around the Mediterranean. From there it must have travelled to South America, because a friend brought up in Brazil with Portuguese maids told me he remembers it from his childhood in Rio. Sixteenth- and seventeenth-century recipe books contain numerous recipes for 'marmalades' using quinces and other fruits, without a trace of oranges and lemons.

It was not until the eighteenth century that oranges began to appear in the recipe as a characteristic feature: the Keiller family had the idea of including strips of orange peel in their conserves, still a famous brand-name to this day. In 1870 a certain Mrs Cooper, a grocer's wife from Oxford, took up making orange marmalade on a commercial scale and created the famous product which epitomizes the British breakfast at its best.

So although many families have their favourite treasured recipes for citrus marmalades, I have chosen some very old country recipes which show their ancestry in the use of unusual fruits and even vegetables.

Cotignac Special

When I was a child, the old quince tree in our Cambridge garden leant dangerously out of a bank and I loved to sit in it where nobody could find me, reading a book. My mother made full use of the crop and every year gleaming jars of this quince jam lined the cold marble shelf in the larder. There is no need to peel the quinces.

MAKES 4.5KG (10LB)
2.7kg (6lb) quinces, sliced
About 300ml (½ pint) water
About 1.8kg (4lb) granulated
   sugar
100g (4oz) whole almonds
100g (4oz) glacé cherries
50g (2oz) chopped mixed peel
450g (1lb) sultanas
50–75g(2–3oz) stem ginger
   (optional)

Place the quinces in a preserving pan and add enough water to just cover. Place them over a gentle heat and cook them to a pulp, about 1 hour. Stir from time to time to prevent them sticking to the bottom and burning. Pass the pulp through a sieve. Weigh the pulp and for every 450g (1lb) add 350g (12oz) sugar. Return to the pan with the almonds and sultanas and cook to a thick purée. Boil until it reaches setting point (see page 140). Add the cherries and peel. Stir in the ginger, if using, cut into tiny cubes. Put into jars while still hot, and when cool cover with waxed paper. Cover and seal, and store in a cool dark place.

Carrot Marmalade

A stunning 'marmalade', delicious on wholemeal granary toast for breakfast. The zing of ginger is superb with the lemony flavour.

MAKES 1.4KG (3LB)
900g (2lb) grated carrots
675g (1½lb) sugar
2 lemons, quartered and sliced
2 teaspoons ground ginger

Cook the carrots with a little water until tender. Add the sugar and stir until dissolved. Add the sliced lemons and cook all together slowly, until the mixture thickens and reaches setting point (see page 140). Pot in warm, clean jars. Cover with waxed discs, and seal. Store in a dark, dry, cool place.

Apricot Marmalade

This thick apricot conserve is made with the kernels added to the mixture, giving their nutty flavour as well as a crunch to the finished product. A great summer favourite, simply delicious with hot croissants. I have not set a quantity because the joy of this recipe is that you can use any quantity you want to as long as you follow the proportions.

Ripe apricots   *Sugar*

Cut the apricots in half and remove the stones. Weigh the fruit and to every 450g (1lb) allow 450g (1lb) sugar. Sprinkle the sugar over the apricots and leave for 12 hours. Break the stones with a nutcracker and blanch the kernels in boiling water for 3–4 minutes.
Put the fruit, sugar and kernels into a preserving pan and simmer very gently until setting point is reached (see page 140) –

about 45 minutes. Remove any scum with a slotted spoon, then pot in clean, warm jars. Cover with waxed discs, seal, and store in a dark, dry cool place.

Tomato and Lemon Marmalade

This highly unusual combination makes a surprisingly delicious 'marmalade'. A tip for lemons: store them in a jar of cold water in the fridge and they keep for weeks. Also, you can freeze cut quarters of lemon in plastic bags.

MAKES 1.4KG (3LB)
12 medium-sized ripe tomatoes, peeled and thinly sliced
450g (1lb) sugar
1½ lemons, quartered and thinly sliced

Put the tomatoes into a preserving pan and bring to a simmer. Cook slowly until they are soft. Add the sugar and stir until dissolved. Add the lemons and continue to cook slowly until thick, stirring from time to time, until setting point is reached (see page 140). Pot in warm, clean jars and cover with waxed discs.

Cotignac is a rich, dark jam made from quinces.

BEES AND HONEY

More flies are caught with honey than with vinegar Dutch proverb

Ever since antiquity the busy bee has been producing the sublime and justly world-famous honey from wild herbs on the slopes of Mount Hymettus in Greece, and the celebrated honey from Mount Hybla in Sicily. 450g (1lb) of honey requires 37.000 bee-loads of nectar, the equivalent of travelling 148.000 miles! Small wonder that bees have inspired mankind with a sense of awe.

Today there is hardly a country in the world that does not produce honey. Together the USA, USSR, China, Central and South America produce 100,000 tons of honey each, a world production of 500,000 tons. Australia and New Zealand are well-known for their honey too: black bees from Europe were thought to have arrived in Australia on the convict ship Isabella in 1822, and missionaries took bees to New Zealand in 1839. In the USA the only indigenous bee, the stingless Meliponinae, was domesticated by the Mayans. Utah now calls itself 'The Beehive State' and the seal of the Mormons, who imported the honey bee there, is a beehive surrounded by flowers beneath the crowning word 'Industry'.

Honey has acquired legendary status. It has been used in ointments, as a taste-killer for medicines, as a cosmetic which softens the skin, and as a disinfectant. Honey was the principal sweetener in cooking until the eighteenth century, although in the Middle East syrup of figs or dates was an alternative. Honey was and is useful as a preservative: it keeps indefinitely because of its high sugar content. The rinsings of the combs were used to make mead, and mead-drinkers were renowned for not only their vigour but for living long and healthy lives. Beeswax has been used in candles, cosmetics and industry, and had many household uses including polish, waterproofing, and sealing bottles. The famous waxworks of Madame Tussauds are made of beeswax, and royal jelly – a hormone which unfortunately decomposes fast outside the hive – has given rise to international beauty legends.

Honey gives energy quickly and is the food most easily absorbed by humans.

Baklavas

Making your own baklavas – those deliciously fragrant Greek pastries (made all the more delicious if you use Hymettus honey) – is nothing like as difficult as you might think.

MAKES 8	Melted butter for brushing
75g (3oz) unsalted butter or margarine	Ground cinnamon
75g (3oz) honey	SYRUP
225g (8oz) walnuts, chopped finely	125ml (4fl oz) honey
	125ml (4fl oz) water
250g (8oz) filo pastry	Juice of ½ lemon

Preheat the oven to 180°C/350°F/gas 4. Heat the butter or margarine with the honey. Add the chopped nuts.

Line a well-buttered 18cm (7in) square baking tin with 3 layers of filo, brushing each one with melted butter. Spread a thin layer of the filling on the pastry, sprinkle with cinnamon and cover with 2 more layers of buttered filo. Repeat, and finish with 3 layers of filo on top. Tuck the ends and sides in to contain the filling. Brush the top with melted butter and score into squares or diamonds with a sharp knife.

Bake until golden and crisp, 25–30 minutes. To make the syrup, boil the honey, water and lemon juice, and while still hot, pour over the baklavas. Leave to cool before cutting into pieces for serving.

Honey Cookies

A month of celebrating, drinking honey-based wines such as mead, metheglin or hydromel, is the source of 'honeymoon'. Attila the Hun greatly overdid the celebrations at his wedding by drinking too much of these potent wines during his honeymoon – and died. These honey cookies however should be safe enough: light, wafery and crisp, they melt in the mouth.

MAKES 18–20	25g (1oz) plain flour
50g (2oz) margarine	Pinch of salt
50g (2oz) demerara sugar	½ teaspoon ground ginger
50g (2oz) honey, melted	A squeeze of lemon juice
50g (2oz) wholemeal flour	

Preheat the oven to 160°C/325°F/gas 3.

Put the margarine, sugar and honey into a pan and stir over a

Honey cookies.

gentle heat until the margarine has melted. Remove from the heat and stir in the flours, salt and ginger. Then stir in the lemon juice.

Place teaspoonfuls of the mixture on a well greased baking tray, allowing room for the biscuits to spread. Bake for 8–10 minutes until they are a light golden brown.

Leave to cool for a minute or two, then carefully lift off and cool on a wire rack.

Honey-baked Figs

From Turkey, here is a dish redolent of Mediterranean sun. Poaching ripe figs in white wine, honey and a little lemon is a gastronomic delight. These are then served cold, covered with a thick layer of whipped cream and sprinkled with toasted almonds.

SERVES 4–6	2 teaspoons lemon juice
450g (1lb) fresh figs	Strip of lemon rind
300ml (½ pint) white wine	300ml (½ pint) whipping cream
4 tablespoons clear honey	25g (1oz) toasted flaked almonds

Preheat the oven to 200°C/400°F/gas 6.

Arrange the figs closely together in a shallow ovenproof dish. Put the wine, honey, lemon juice and rind into a pan and heat gently until the honey has dissolved. Pour over the figs. Cover and bake until tender, about 10–15 minutes depending on the ripeness of the figs. Remove from the oven and leave to cool.

WILD FOOD CALENDAR

The food-for-free season starts in spring with blossoms and young leaves and the spring crop of mushrooms. Throughout the summer you can pick a wide range of greens, herbs and flowers with which to make salads, cordials, pies and ice-creams. Come the autumn the harvest becomes a serious business with the plentiful annual yields of berries, nuts, mushrooms and fruits that cloak the autumn hedgerows and fields. This calendar is a general guide to how you can make the most of the wild harvest by freezing or storing seasonal foods. It also gives advice on which plants are available at which times of the year.

For the Freezer
soups, quiches and pies, tarts, ice-creams, cakes and cookies, sauces, sorbets, gratins

For the Storecupboard
cordials, preserves in brandy, vinegars, teas and tisanes, dried mushrooms

For the larder
jams, jellies, chutneys, ketchups, wines, cheeses and butters, pickles, curds, syrups, relishes

Spring

alexanders
birch
bistort
chickweed
comfrey
corn salad
crab-apple blossom

dandelion
garlic mustard
hawthorn blossom
mushrooms
nettles
violets
wild garlic

Summary

Summer

angelica	mint
bittercress	nasturtium
borage	nettle
camomile	plantain
chives	purslane
clary	rose petals
comfrey	salad burnet
corn salad	seakale
deadnettle	sorrel
fat hen	sow thistle
elderflowers	tansy
good King Henry	thyme
lady's mantle	watercress
lime	wild raspberry
mallow	wild strawberry
marigold	yarrow
marjoram	
marsh samphire	
meadowsweet	

Autumn

bilberry	dewberry
blackberry	elderberry
bullace	juniper
cherry	medlar
chestnut	mushroom
cloudberry	rowan
cobnut	sloe
crab-apple	walnut
cranberry	winter cress

Blackberry-and-apple tarte tatin.

WILD FOOD THROUGH THE SEASONS

The long tradition of gathering wild food is associated mainly with autumn when fruits and berries mature in the hedgerows, and a feast of fungi is to be found in the woods. However, there are many spring shoots and summer leaves that make excellent ingredients too, offering a rich wild harvest for free: country walks through the seasons can furnish you with baskets full of tasty and unusual flavours. I took to 'hedgerow cookery', as I call it, when I first moved to the countryside from the city in my twenties. It seemed like a dream come true to be wandering the lanes and fields instead of trailing around a supermarket. This selection of dishes, both savoury and sweet, are favourites among the many that I have used over the years to make the most of the wild harvest.

Blackberry-and-apple Tart Tatin

Blackberry-and-apple is one of the longest-lasting marriages in gastronomy. This upside-down version is inspired by a French classic, and is divine.

SERVES 4

450g (1lb) blackberries

225g (8oz) apples, peeled, cored and sliced

50g (2oz) caster sugar

Pinch of ground cinnamon

225g (8oz) puff pastry

Milk for brushing

Preheat the oven to 220°C/425°F/gas 7.

Mix the blackberries with the apples and sugar and a pinch of cinnamon. Put into a 25cm (10in) pie dish. Roll out the puff pastry to a circle measuring 1cm (½in) larger than the rim, and place it over the top. Brush with milk. Bake for 25–30 minutes, until the top is risen and golden.

To serve, flip it upside down on to a serving plate. Cut into wedges and serve immediately, with thick Greek yogurt to pass around.

Comfrey and Wild Mushroom Puffs

Majestic comfrey with its beautiful bell-shaped flowers contains all the mineral richness of spinach, plus vitamin B12 – the only vegetable to do so – and also has a high protein content. Gather it from June onwards, usually from damp shady places. Wild mushrooms grow freely from spring through to autumn: the Romans deemed them food for the gods.

SERVES 4 (makes 8 triangles)	225g (8oz) wild mushrooms such as chanterelles, puffballs, ceps, sliced
450g (1lb) cooked comfrey leaves (900g/2lb fresh), drained	50g (2oz) butter
	2 garlic cloves, crushed
300ml (½ pint) béchamel sauce (see below)	2 teaspoons dried mixed herbs
	450g (1lb) puff pastry

Mix the cooked comfrey with the béchamel. Sauté the sliced mushrooms in the butter until soft, then stir in the crushed garlic and herbs. Leave to cool for 5 minutes, then drain off the juices. Add the mushrooms to the comfrey mixture.

Preheat the oven to 200°C/400°F/gas 6. Roll out the pastry and cut into 8 x 12cm (5in) triangles. Place a tablespoon or so of the mixture in the centre of each. Moisten the edges of the pastry and fold over one corner. Press the edges together firmly with a fork. Brush with beaten egg and bake for 25 minutes until risen and golden brown.

Chickweed Sandwiches

One of the great surprises of wild food is how delicious chickweed is. It is such an abundant and common weed, found much of the year round from Greenland to Tierra del Fuego, Lapland to Capetown, Siberia to Tasmania. It makes a stunning summer soup as well as being delicious in salad, and makes a highly nutritious drink when juiced as my friends in Pennsylvania do. In sandwiches, it tastes not unlike watercress, a delicate version.

Wash the chickweed leaves, and chop them a little. Lightly spread slices of fresh granary bread with a mixture of cream cheese and softened butter, and place the leaves between the slices, adding a little lemon juice if you like. Cut off the crusts and cut into four small squares.

Samphire with Melted Butter

Marsh samphire or glasswort (*Salicornea europaea*) is a succulent annual to be found on mud flats around European coastlines and along river estuaries. Equipped with waterproof boots and large plastic bags – it grows in huge abundance – you can gather this muddy harvest at low tide. It is definitely worth it: samphire is in my view worthy of being rated a kind of sea asparagus. Serve with melted butter and you have a dish fit for a king.

Wash the samphire well. Cook it – roots and all – in boiling water for 10 minutes. Serve on a hot plate, since it loses its heat very quickly. Holding the root, dip the fleshy leaves into melted butter (to which you can add a little crushed garlic or a few drops of fresh lemon juice) and strip the fleshy part off the stem. Alternatively you can wait until it is cold, and use it in salads and sandwiches.

Béchamel Sauce

MAKES ¾ PINT (450ML)	450ml (¾ pint) milk
40g (1½oz) plain flour	Salt and white pepper
40g (1½oz) butter or margarine	Pinch of nutmeg (optional)

Put all the ingredients into a heavy-based saucepan and whisk continuously with a wire whisk until the mixture thickens and is smooth. Bring to the boil and simmer gently for 5 minutes to allow the flour to cook, stirring with a wooden spoon. Season to taste with salt and pepper and a pinch of nutmeg if desired.

Garlic Crisp of Nettles and Mushrooms

Nettles grow almost everywhere and have been used by the country housewife for generations, both in cooking and in herbal practices. They make a superlative soup, which you can make just as you would spinach soup. So abundant and common are they that there is nothing to stop you picking masses of nettles from spring onwards – with rubber gloves on of course. Pick the top shoots – the top six leaves – for the most tender flavour.

SERVES 4	CRUMBLE
900g (2lb) nettle tops	100g (4oz) breadcrumbs
225g (8oz) mushrooms, sliced	2 garlic cloves, crushed
3 tablespoons olive oil	50g (2oz) grated cheese
300ml (½ pint) béchamel	25g (1oz) butter, diced small
sauce (see page 151)	Salt and pepper
Salt, pepper and a little nutmeg	

Preheat the oven to 180°C/350°F/gas 4.

Wash the nettles and cook like spinach, just with the water on the leaves. Drain well. Sauté the mushrooms in the oil. Fold both into the béchamel and mix thoroughly. Season to taste with salt, pepper and a little nutmeg. Place in a baking dish.

Mix the crumble ingredients together, season, and sprinkle over the nettle mixture. Bake for 40 minutes, until the topping is crisp. Serve hot.

Cranberry Relish

From a friend in New York, this adaptation of a traditional Thanksgiving relish shows how multi-cultural influences have integrated within much western cooking: Mexican, Canadian, Indian, Mediterranean tastes all add to the humble New England cranberry. This makes a serious amount, for a large party at the very least, and any leftovers freeze well.

450g (1lb) fresh cranberries	2 jalapeño chillies, deseeded
Rind of 1 orange, grated	2 tablespoons maple syrup
1 orange, peeled and segmented	2 tablespoons grated root ginger

Put the cranberries into a blender with all the other ingredients and process to a purée. Serve with roast turkey, but it is also delicious with pre-dinner nibbles.

Almond Plum Tart

My neighbour has a Victoria plum tree in her garden which I love to use for this recipe each autumn. The golden-brown crust of almonds which tops the plums in a light pastry case makes for an irresistible dessert. She doesn't possess a rolling pin: she rolls her pastry out with a wine bottle filled with chilled water which, she swears, keeps the pastry light.

SERVES 6	1 egg white, lightly beaten
150g (5oz) ground almonds	450g (1lb) plums, halved and
75g (3oz) caster sugar, plus	stoned
extra for sprinkling	Pinch of cinnamon
225g (8oz) shortcrust pastry	A little butter or margarine

Preheat the oven to 200°C/400°F/gas 6.

Mix together the ground almonds and sugar. Roll out the pastry and use to line a 20cm (8in) flan case. Brush with lightly beaten egg white – this is a useful tip given to me by a WI cook, to stop the pastry going soggy. Sprinkle one-third of the ground almond mixture over the pastry to form a thick layer. Place the plums on top and add a little sugar. Spread the rest of the almond mixture over the top and dot with butter or margarine. Bake at the bottom of the oven for 35–40 minutes, covering it with a piece of foil after 10–15 minutes, to prevent the almonds burning. The pastry base will cook crisp by remaining on the oven floor.

Season of mists and mellow fruitfulness,
Close bosom-friend of the maturing sun;
Conspiring with him how to load and bless
With fruits the vines that round the thatch-eves run;
To bend with apples the moss'd cottage-trees,
And fill all fruit with ripeness to the core;
To swell the gourd, and plump the hazel shells
With a sweet kernel; to set budding more,
And still more, later flowers for the bees,
Until they think warm days will never cease,
For Summer has o'er-brimm'd their clammy cells.

John Keates *To Autumn* (1819)

Sorrel picked from the wild makes an elegant summer soufflé.

French Sorrel Soufflé

Wild sorrel can be found in grassy places and banks. The Laplanders use it instead of rennet – its sourness curdles milk. Its name comes from an old French word meaning 'sour', and it found its culinary way into refreshingly sharp sauces to go with rich meats. It makes a stunning soup or soufflé. This one is based on a classic French recipe.

SERVES 4

350g (12oz) fresh sorrel

150ml (¼ pint) béchamel
  sauce (see page 151)

50g (2oz) grated Gruyère cheese

4 large eggs, separated

Black pepper

A little sea salt

Preheat the oven to 190°C/375°F/gas 5. Wash the sorrel and cook like spinach, just with the water on the leaves, for 3–4 minutes. Drain thoroughly. Mix into the béchamel with the cheese, and season to taste. Cool a little, then stir in the well beaten egg yolks. Beat the egg whites until very stiff, then fold in carefully. Pour into a buttered soufflé dish and bake for 25–30 minutes, until risen and golden, and still slightly moist in the centre when a clean sharp knife is inserted. Serve immediately.

WILD MUSHROOMS

The incomparable thrill of mushrooming is akin to a treasure hunt. The place: the silence and stillness of the autumn woods, or the early-morning fields as a low sun struggles through gentle mist. The scene: falling leaves, the smell of damp ground, that first chill in the air as summer relinquishes its hold.

Mushroom-hunting is pretty well a global pursuit: fungi have no respect for boundaries and spring up abundantly wherever conditions are right. So the woods of Russia, the USA, China and Europe all have their secret harvests hidden away for the delight of the enthusiast. Even the desert gives up treasure: the Kalahari in Botswana contains some of the richest truffle harvests of the world.

Mushrooms are best gathered into smooth woven baskets – the purpose-made ones are flat, so as not to damage the delicate flesh of the fungi. If you are going to eat your wild mushrooms fresh, cover them with damp paper as soon as you get them home, and store in the fridge until you are ready to cook them.

Sweet and Sour Mushrooms

There are two hundred meatless days required by the Russian Orthodox calendar, and this is when the mushroom comes into its own. Fresh or dried, pickled or salted, they provide both protein and a satisfaction-factor in the absence of meat. My friends in Moscow gave me this dish one autumn, using fresh wood oyster mushrooms from their dacha in the country. A delicious way of cooking mushrooms, served cold as a starter or as a light snack.

SERVES 2

175g (6oz) wild mushrooms such as chanterelles, boletus, field mushrooms, and so on
3 tablespoons each olive oil and tarragon vinegar
2 tablespoons sugar
2 cloves
1 bay leaf
Salt
150ml (¼ pint) soured cream

Wipe the mushrooms clean and slice. Heat the oil with the vinegar, sugar, cloves, bay leaf and a pinch of salt, and simmer over a low heat for 5 minutes. Add the mushrooms and simmer, covered, for 3 minutes, stirring from time to time. Leave to cool, then mix in the soured cream. Serve with blinis, little Russian pancakes, to mop up the juice.

Easy Mushroom Curry

When field mushrooms are so abundant that you are hard-pressed to know what to cook next, this is a useful option. I wouldn't use chanterelles or ceps, because of their delicate flavour, but the honest taste of puffballs or oyster mushrooms, or even beefsteak fungus (see page 156) all lend themselves to this simple dish. Easy to make, using garam masala paste, this is a wonderful warming dish for an autumn evening as the weather grows chilly.

Before eating wild mushrooms, always check with a good field guide, or ask an expert.

SERVES 3–4	*1 large bunch fresh coriander*
50g (2oz) butter	*4 canned tomatoes with their juice*
2 large onions, chopped	*450g (1lb) wild mushrooms,*
2 teaspoons garam masala paste	*chopped*
1–2 teaspoons each ground ginger	*Salt*
and turmeric	*1 tablespoon lemon juice*

Melt the butter in a pan, add the onions and spices, cover and cook over a gentle heat for about 10 minutes, until soft. Add the chopped coriander and the tomatoes with their juices, and stir well. Add the mushrooms and mix in well. Season with salt and lemon juice, and cook for 8–10 minutes.

Serve with basmati rice and papadoms.

Fungi alla Crema

This recipe was given to me by an Italian woman living in the Tuscan hills near Florence. She told me how her father had shown her where her grandparents before him had hunted for ceps and chanterelles, following the time-honoured tradition of keeping secret the best places for mushroom hunting. The Italians, she said, take it all with the seriousness it merits, holding numerous festivals in the villages and towns to show off their treasures, a staggering array of many varieties of wild mushrooms neatly stacked in woven baskets lined with the leaves of the sweet chestnut tree.

SERVES 4–6	*Sea salt and freshly ground black*
75g (3oz) butter	*pepper*
900g (2lb) assorted wild	*300ml (½ pint) single cream*
mushrooms	
1 medium bunch fresh tarragon,	
chopped finely	

Melt the butter in a pan, add the mushrooms and stew over a gentle heat, covered, for 10 minutes or until they are soft. Add all but 1 tablespoon of the chopped tarragon and season to taste. Turn up the heat a little and allow to bubble, to evaporate off some of the liquid, then add the cream and bring back to a simmer. Stir well, bubbling, for a further 2 minutes, then serve in individual dishes with the remaining chopped tarragon sprinkled over the top.

Delicious with warm ciabatta bread to mop up the juices.

Oyster mushrooms.

Identifying Fungi

There are people around the world who take great pride in their expertise in identifying fungi. The Aborigines for example have a vast knowledge of wild plants and fungi, and know which ones are dangerous. You need to be absolutely sure of correctly identifying the mushrooms you pick from the wild: you cannot be too careful since eating some fungi can have fatal results, and death by mushroom poisoning is spectacularly unpleasant. Never eat a mushroom unless you are one hundred per cent sure of which one it is. The following fungi are easily identifiable and completely safe to eat: but always check with a field guide before you do so, or consult an expert.

Beefsteak fungus (*Fistulina hepatica*)

Blewits (*Lepista nuda/saevum*)

Boletus/Cep (*Boletus edulis*)

Chanterelle (*Cantherellus cibarius/tubiformis*)

Fairy ring/ Horse/Field mushroom (*Agaricus campestris*)

Horn of Plenty (*Craterellus cornucopioides*)

Parasol mushroom (*Lepiota procera*)

Puffballs (*Lycoperdon* spp.)

Oyster mushrooms (*Pleurotus ostreatus*)

Shaggy ink cap (not with alcohol) (*Coprinus comatus*)

Deep-fried Puffballs

If you are lucky enough to find puffballs in the fields in late summer, this is one of the most delicious ways of cooking them. Mouthwatering, crisp and irresistible. Serve them as soon as possible after cooking, with a little soy sauce to dip them into.

SERVES 4

Fritter batter (see page 132)

1 medium puffball

Wipe the puffball clean and cut into cubes about 1cm (½ in) square. Dip in the fritter batter and deep-fry in very hot oil until the batter is crisp and browned. Drain on kitchen paper and cool a little before serving.

Stuffed Mushrooms

I made these after an expedition to a field on the Welsh borders early one misty morning: large field mushrooms were thick on the ground where none had been visible the evening before. One of the intriguing characteristics of this mysterious creature – neither plant nor animal but microbe – is how it appears so suddenly, as if by a miracle, from nowhere. I filled my basket to overflowing and made this very simple recipe for supper, a delicious meal with a crisp salad, warm granary bread and a glass of red wine.

SERVES 4

4 very large, or 8 medium, flat mushrooms
50g (2oz) breadcrumbs
3 tablespoons milk
40g (1½oz) butter

1 large onion, chopped
1 large garlic clove, crushed
2 tablespoons parsley, chopped
Salt, pepper and a pinch of cayenne (optional)
Grated Parmesan cheese

Preheat the oven to 220°C/425°F/gas 7.

Cut the stalks off the mushrooms and chop them finely. Soak the breadcrumbs in the milk. Melt the butter in a pan, add the onion and cook, covered, for 10 minutes, until soft and translucent. Add the crushed garlic and the chopped stalks, and stir well for a couple of minutes longer. Then add the breadcrumbs and the parsley. Season to taste with salt and pepper and cayenne. Pile the stuffing into the mushroom caps, sprinkle with Parmesan and bake for 15–20 minutes.

Wild mushrooms provide rich feasts to be had from spring through to autumn.

PUDDINGS, CAKES AND COOKIES

Autumnal puddings and cakes made with the annual glut have a special appeal. Our grandmothers the world over made the most of nature's harvest, and much of this 'food for free' has become legendary. My mother's gardener Mr Williams used to say that after a frosty winter there would be a good fruit harvest, and his advice was to pick the crops at full moon, so that the fruit would not lose its plumpness. He also used to swear that wallflowers planted around an apple tree made it fruit better.

Windfall Cake with Nuts

'An apple a day keeps the doctor away', goes an ancient saying. A good excuse to eat this wonderful cake as your apples drop on to the grass and the evenings draw in. To help turn it out – and other moist cakes like it – place a strip of foil across the bottom of the cake tin before putting the mixture in, and this keeps the centre intact as you invert it.

SERVES 8–10

225g (8oz) self-raising flour
Pinch of salt
175g (6oz) butter or margarine
100g (4oz) caster sugar
100g (4oz) hazelnuts or walnut pieces, chopped
350g (12oz) windfall apples, peeled, cored and diced
2 eggs, beaten
Caster sugar for dredging

Preheat the oven to 180°C/350°F/gas 4.

Sift the flour with the salt into a large bowl, then rub in the butter until it resembles breadcrumbs. Stir in the sugar and the nuts, then fold in the apples. Stir in the eggs with a metal spoon until thoroughly amalgamated. Pour the mixture into a deep, greased 20cm (8in) cake tin. Bake for 50 minutes, or until a skewer inserted into the centre comes out clean. Leave to cool in the tin for 10–15 minutes, then invert on to a wire rack. Remove the tin and leave for a further 30 minutes. Dredge the top with caster sugar and serve warm.

Windfall cake with nuts.

Blackberry Bread and Butter Pudding

Misty mornings, low clear sunlight casting long shadows over the fields – and it is blackberrying time again. This is an autumnal version of summer pudding, as described to me by a friend in the village who is a keen Women's Institute cook. It is sensational.

SERVES 6

675 g (1½lb) blackberries

Squeeze of lemon juice

75–100g (3–4oz) sugar to taste

1 teaspoon cinnamon

10–12 slices of bread, crusts removed

Butter for greasing

Cook the blackberries with a very little water over a gentle heat, just until the juice runs. Add the lemon juice, sugar and cinnamon and cook until they soften. Cool.

Butter the bread lightly on one side. Line a bowl with the slices, buttered side outwards, and fill with the blackberries plus enough of their juices to moisten the bread. Cover the top with more slices of bread. Press down with a plate, put a weight on top and chill in the fridge for several hours or overnight.

Turn out on a platter and cut into wedges. Serve with thick yogurt or cream.

Best Walnut Cake

If you soak fresh walnuts in salted water overnight they will be easier to crack, and the flesh will come out whole. If you are using dry ones which taste a bit stale, cover them with boiling water, drain, then put on a baking sheet in a low oven for 20 minutes.

SERVES 10–12

200g (7oz) plain flour

1 teaspoon baking powder

200g (7oz) unsalted butter

200g (7oz) caster sugar

3 large eggs

75g (3oz) chopped walnuts

Preheat the oven to 170°C/325°F/gas 3

Sift the flour with the baking powder. Cream the butter with the sugar, then beat in the eggs one at a time until the mixture is fluffy. Fold in the flour and add the chopped walnuts. Mix well.

Bake in a greased 20cm (8in) cake tin for 30–40 minutes. Cool for 10 minutes on a wire rack, then remove from the tin and allow to cool completely. Ice with coffee icing.

Apple Dumplings

My neighbour's tip to ripen apples: put them into a brown paper bag with one already-ripe apple, pierce a few holes in the bag and store in a cool dark place for 24 hours.

SERVES 4

4 baking apples (preferably Bramleys)

225g (8oz) blackberries

Sugar to taste

½ teaspoon each ground cinnamon and ginger

450g (1lb) shortcrust pastry

1 egg, beaten

Preheat the oven to 190°C/375°F/gas 5.

Core the apples and cut the centre out to make a good-sized hole. Mix the blackberries with a little sugar to taste, and the spices, and pack into the centre of the apples. Roll out the pastry and cut into 4 large squares. Place an apple in the centre of each square, and bring opposite corners together. Moisten with cold water and pinch the edges so that they stick. Do the same with the other 2 corners. Pinch the edges together and brush the pastry with beaten egg. Bake for 25–30 minutes, until the pastry is golden and the apples inside soft. Lovely with thick yogurt, or English custard (see page 131).

Cobnut Cookies

Irresistibly crunchy, these cookies come from the country kitchen of an American living in Normandy, where the annual crop of wild cobnuts is abundant.

MAKES 12–14

225g (8oz) plain flour

75g (3oz) caster sugar

150g (5oz) margarine or

butter, softened plus extra for greasing

100g (4oz) cobnuts, finely chopped

Sift the flour with the sugar. Rub the softened butter or margarine into the flour until the mixture resembles fine breadcrumbs. Mix in the nuts, and knead to a soft, smooth dough on a wooden board. Roll into a sausage shape about 5cm (2 in) across, and chill for 1–2 hours.

Preheat the oven to 180°C/350°F/gas 4.

Cut the roll into 5 mm (¼ in) slices and place on a well-greased baking sheet. Bake for 15 minutes until lightly browned. Cool on a wire rack.

Plum Cobbler

This is my slightly unorthodox version of a traditional cobbler that my American mother always used to make, as her mother had taught her in their home in the glorious woods of Pennsylvania.

SERVES 6	40g (1½oz) soft brown sugar
40g (1½oz) butter or margarine	900g (2lb) plums
	A little grated lemon rind

Melt the butter or margarine and pour into an 20cm (8in) cake tin. Sprinkle the sugar over the top. Stone the plums, cut into quarters lengthwise and arrange in the bottom of the tin with the lemon rind.

TOPPING	225g (8oz) flour
75g (3oz) butter or margarine	2 teaspoons baking powder
150g (5oz) sugar	1 teaspoon cinnamon
1 egg, beaten	Pinch of salt
	250ml (8fl oz) milk

Preheat the oven to 180°C/350°F/gas 4.

To make the topping, cream the butter and sugar and add the beaten egg. Sift together the flour, baking powder, cinnamon and salt and stir it gradually with the milk in to the butter mixture to make a smooth batter. Spread this batter over the plums and bake for 30–35 minutes, until a knife plunged into the centre comes out clean. Allow to cool a little on a wire rack before cutting into squares and serving with thick yogurt or custard.

Wild Strawberry or Raspberry Vacherin

The extremely delicate flavour of wild strawberries makes it one of our most sought-after wild fruits, and I grow a patch in my herb garden to provide me with its inimitable fruits. Likewise, if you find wild raspberries growing, try them in this superb vacherin once prepared for me by my French friend Emanuele.

SERVES 6	FOR THE FILLING
MERINGUES	225g (8oz) wild strawberries
2 egg whites	or raspberries, hulled
100g (4oz) caster sugar	300 ml (½ pint) crème fraîche
A few drops vanilla essence	2 tablespoons caster sugar
A few drops lemon juice	1 egg white

Preheat the oven to 130°C/250°F/gas ½.

To make the meringues, beat the egg whites until they are stiff, then gradually beat in the sugar with the vanilla and lemon until they are thick and shiny and hold their shape. Place 12 tablespoon blobs on a well-greased tin and bake for 1 hour. Leave in the oven to cool, with the door ajar, overnight.

Mash the strawberries and fold into the crème fraîche with all their juices. Stir in the sugar. Beat the egg white stiffly and fold it in.

To serve, place 2 meringues on either side of each dish, and spoon the filling in between. Serve at once.

Spicy Pecan Cookies

Pecans are native to the Mississippi valley and neighbouring states, and are the richest and oiliest of all the nuts – and in some people's view the most delectable. On a trip to New Orleans my daughter came across this, the ultimate American recipe: maple syrup with chopped pecans added, to go with ice-cream. A glorious idea, served up with these cookies.

MAKES 12–14	
100g (4oz) plain flour	1 teaspoon mixed spice
75g (3oz) caster sugar	3 tablespoons oats
65g (2½oz) soft butter or margarine	50g (2oz) pecan halves

Preheat the oven to 180°C/350°F/gas 4.

Sift the flour and put in a bowl with the sugar, butter and spice. Mix thoroughly with your fingertips until it resembles breadcrumbs, then knead until smooth on a wooden board. Divide into 12–14 pieces and roll into small balls. Spread out the oats on a plate. Press the balls into the oats, making a flat circle 7.5cm (3in) in diameter, so that they are covered in oats on both sides. Press 2 pecan halves into the top of each one. Cook for 15–18 minutes, until lightly browned. Lift out while still warm and cool on a wire rack.

Mississippi Sundae

PER PERSON	3–4 tablespoons pure maple syrup
3 scoops vanilla ice-cream	1 tablespoon pecan nuts, chopped and toasted

Put the ice-cream scoops into a tall glass and scatter with the nuts. Pour the maple syrup over the top to serve.

Blueberry bake (above) and Blueberry slice (below).

SERVES 8	4 large eggs
225g (8oz) white bread with the crusts cut off, cut into tiny cubes	150 ml (¼ pint) maple syrup
Butter for greasing	300 ml (½ pint) milk
200g (7oz) light cream cheese, cut into tiny cubes	2 teaspoons ground cinnamon
	1–2 tablespoons sugar

Arrange half of the bread cubes in a buttered 20cm (8in) soufflé dish. Scatter with the cream cheese, then sprinkle the blueberries over it. Arrange the remaining bread cubes over the top.

Beat the eggs to a froth, then continue to beat with the maple syrup and milk, adding the cinnamon. Pour the mixture evenly over the bread and press down with a plate over the top. Chill for several hours or overnight, so that the juices are absorbed into the bread. Preheat the oven to 180°C/350°F/gas 4. Just before baking, sprinkle the top thickly with sugar, and bake for 60 minutes, until puffed and golden brown. Eat either hot, warm or cold, with cream or yogurt.

Blueberry Slice

If you live in Europe you are more likely to find bilberries than blueberries, but you can use either for this recipe. Blueberries are bigger and juicier, very common in parts of the United States, and they make wonderful cakes, muffins, sorbets and pies. This scrumptious treat is delicious served with thick yogurt.

SERVES 6	150g (5oz) soft brown sugar
150g (5oz) softened butter or margarine, plus extra for greasing	200g (7oz) oats
	75g (3oz) flour
	250g (8oz) blueberries

Blueberry Bake

Blueberries and bilberries (*Vaccinium myrtillus* and *V. angustifolia*) are one of the first wild fruits of the season. From the mountains of West Maryland in the USA comes this unusual and delectable dessert, given to me by a woman who runs a bed and breakfast business there and who cooks evening meals for her clients. This is an established favourite, and no wonder.

Preheat the oven to 190°C/325°F/gas 5. Place the butter, sugar, oats and flour in a bowl and rub together until evenly mixed. Press half of the mixture into the bottom of a 450g (1lb) greased loaf tin. Cover with the blueberries. Press the remaining mixture over the top and press down lightly. Bake for 30–35 minutes until lightly browned, cool on a wire rack. Loosen the edges while still warm, then turn out when completely cold. Cut into slices to serve.

CUPS
AND THEIR
CUSTOMS

Wine has come to symbolize full communion with life, as sung by Edward Fitzgerald in *Rubaiyat of Omar Khayyam*:

Awake, my little ones, and fill the Cup
Before Life's Liquor in its Cup be dry.

T he vine is an age-old symbol of peace and prosperity. Wine was cultivated by the ancient Persians, and enjoyed by the Egyptians, who also used it in temple rituals and who believed that Osiris was the first god to make wine. The Greeks went on to develop the fine art of wine-making, and thus it took root in western civilization. Plato recommended it as 'a comfortable medicine against the dryness of old age, that we might renew our youth'. The Romans took their wine-making skills all over Europe as their empire increased, and today most of the world's wine is produced in Italy, France, Spain, Germany, Argentina, Algeria, Russia, Australia, New Zealand, South Africa, USA and Portugal. The 'blood of the grape' still retains its ancient sacrificial origins in the communion service of the Christian church, a spiritual drink which was also, in ancient times and in differing cultures, offered to the dead as a revivifying force.

The 'fruit of Dionysus', god of wine and worshipped by some as Lord of souls, is widely illustrated in myth as a symbol of a happier life in the other world. Dionysus represents the productive abundance and intoxicating power of nature which transforms man from his usual grey way of living, stimulating his mystical faculties which are habitually subdued by the trivial concerns of living. The Hebrews gave credit to Noah who, having discovered the delights of the grape, carried several young vines to safety with him on the Ark. To Noah was ascribed the wisdom that man, before drinking wine, is as gentle as a lamb. When he drinks moderately, he becomes as brave and as strong as a lion. When he drinks to excess he resembles a swine.

Wine harvests throughout the world are an occasion for celebration, and every country has their tradition. In France, the *vendange* takes place in late September with hired workers who are given simple meals in the spirit of a bacchanal: a *pot au feu* and local cheeses washed down with the regional wine. In Spain the *vendimia* is marked by flamenco dancing and singing, and tapas offered as refreshment. The *Weinlese* in Germany offers public tastings, and in Hungary traditions which go back hundreds of years were unchanged at the beginning of this century. The Tokay harvest – Hungary's inimitable honey-sweet wine – was accompanied by the music of gypsy fiddlers, and the workers are rewarded with a paprika goulash and stuffed cabbage, washed down with peach brandy. A huge and heavy bouquet of grapes was carried on a pole by two men leading a festive procession. In Italy the *vendemmia* workers were rewarded with a pasta soup, boiled stuffed beef or roast chicken or both, and tomato and radicchio salad.

Joy is our greatest asset, just as fear ever was and still is our greatest curse .... The wine instinct is the natural urge for joy. The joy that is wine is the joy of sunshine. It has nothing in common with the many drugs and poisons which some people crave for and turn to in their search for peace of mind or relief from frayed nerves. Wine is not a drug, it never is a craving and rarely becomes a habit .... Wine is a symbol and it is an instinct, Man's time-honoured urge for joy.

André Simon *Let Wine Be Mine* (1946)

CEREMONIAL CUPS

Frequent cups prolong the rich repast
Alexander Pope, *The Rape of the Lock* (1714)

Grace Cup

The grace cup was reputed to have been devised by Margaret Atheling, wife of Malcolm Canmore, King of Scotland, to induce the Scots to remain at table for grace to be said. It was filled with the choicest wines, and each guest was allowed to drink as much as he wanted as the cup was passed around after the saying of grace.

Early drinking cups were made of gold or silver by master craftsmen, and elaborately decorated with precious stones or fine chasing. The Howard Grace Cup in the Victoria and Albert Museum in London is made of ivory set in gold with the inscription: *Drink thy wine with joy.* The London City Companies possess fine grace or loving cups for use at their banquets, some of them with four handles, and typically filled with a mixture of wine and spices or sack, to be drunk according to the loving-cup ritual.

Loving Cup

Loving cups go back to the pagan custom of wassailing (see page 169). As Christianity spread the monks renamed the cup 'poculum caritatis', or Loving Cup. The custom still remains at state banquets, City of London company dinners, and in some of the university colleges. A loving cup is still served at St Catherine's College Cambridge at the Commemoration Feast of the college's foundation in 1474, in a ceremony dating from the seventeenth century. The recipe is a mixture of 1½ litres (2½ pints) each of white wine and sparkling wine and ¼ bottle of Cointreau or Curaçao

Four two-handled cups made of silver, of great antiquity and value, are used to serve the loving cup towards the end of the feast, passed around clockwise. When the head of the table rises to drink, his neighbours to left and right also rise. The drinker bows to them, first to right and then to left, with the toast to the Founders. Bowing to your neighbours keeps the right or dagger hand employed, rendering you defenceless, so the name 'loving' cup therefore took on a secular symbolism, that of guarding your friend who was drinking from harm: a bonding ritual in the masonic tradition.

The man with the loving cup (for this is essentially a male ritual) then drinks and the other two turn their backs to protect him from attack: using both his hands precludes him from drawing his sword in self-defence. With another bow he passes the cup to his left-hand neighbour. As soon as the right-hand neighbour sits, the person on the left of the left-hand neighbour rises so that there are still three people standing, the centre one of whom holds the cup. And so the cup circulates around the table, a napkin around the right handle of the cup.

The loving cup.

Good glass should be fine not coarse, perfectly clean and well-polished.

The libation varied: sometimes the beverage was 'sack', sometimes a spiced wine. Sack was a wine imported from Spain and the Canaries, usually sherry or malaga. An eighteenth century record tells how at Temple Bar the loving cup was strictly observed and that only one draught was allowed per person. At one feast however, 36 quarts (72 pints) of the liquor were consumed by 70 people ...

If sacke and sugar be a fault, God help the wicked
William Shakespeare *Henry IV. part i* (1589–90)

Glasses

The shape, size and colour of wine glasses can make or break the appreciation of good wine: a good glass should be fine, plain, perfectly clean and well-polished. Wash in hot soapy water, then rinse under hot water then cold before setting upside down to drain. When dry, polish with a soft cloth until crystal clear. Glass retains smells of all sorts and these can easily affect the flavour of the wine. Ideally, it should be large enough to hold a fair measure of wine when only half full, and curved in at the top to retain the bouquet.

'Lamb's Wool' is a traditional English country drink made with apples and spices.

CELEBRATORY CUPS

There was laughing and chattering, and 'pass the cup round',
Bargains and toasts and rounds, and so till Evensong.
Wilham Langland *The Vision of Piers Plowman*, c. 1367

Rural traditions are rich in celebratory cups: special brews to mark particular festivals have been going for centuries, and many rural areas of Europe continue these customs that give rural life its vitality and individuality. Celebratory wine cups used to be part and parcel of feasting, near-lethal libations passed around with traditional rituals to drink a health or a toast. The term 'toast' probably derived from the seventeenth-century custom of floating a piece of toast spread with nutmeg or other spices on top, to give the wine flavour. Yet drinking a toast in company also has a sinister origin, which comes from triumphing over your enemy: a cup or goblet containing drink was called the skull or skoll, from the barbarous Nordic practice of converting the skull of an enemy into a drinking cup. Hence the toast: 'skoll'.

Lamb's Wool

This country Christmas drink is made with baked apples in strong ale, spiced with nutmeg and ginger, and sweetened with raw sugar. It was made in earthenware vessels and was originally dedicated to the angel presiding over fruits and seeds. Some friends in the west country still make it every winter to an original recipe and for them Christmas would not be the same without it.

PER PERSON	½ teaspoon ground nutmeg
2 apples, quartered	1 teaspoon groud ginger
600ml (1 pint) beer	100g (4oz) brown sugar

Preheat the oven to 180°C/350°F/gas mark 4.

Cut the apple quarters crosswise and put into a metal tray and bake for 30 minutes. Warm the beer gently and add the spices and sugar. Stir until dissolved, about 3–4 minutes, being careful not to overheat. Float the apples on top and it is ready to serve.

Wassail Cup

Wassailing the apple trees is a pagan ceremony to bring good crops and good fortune to the house. *Waeshael* means 'be whole, be well' and the ceremony was enacted around the New Year. A wassail song was sung, a wassail cup of spiced ale drunk, then pieces of toast were dipped in the drink and placed in the fork of the tree. Shotguns were fired through the branches to frighten off evil spirits, or trays banged to make a loud noise. Toasts were drunk to the tree as if it were a person.

This is what they would drink, from Sir Watkin William Wynne's recipe dated 1722:

Put into a quart of warm beer one pound of raw sugar, on which grate a nutmeg and some ginger; then add four glasses of sherry and two quarts more of beer, with three slices of lemon; add more sugar, if required, and serve it with three slices of toasted bread floating in it.

It is traditionally served with hot baked apples floating on top.

Glogg

This mulled wine from Sweden keeps out the winter cold, and is a popular drink for parties and celebrations around Christmas.

A Norwegian version, called Skrub, was sent to me by a friend. This is made more simply, with cinnamon infused in water and sugar, then added to brandy, heated again and this mixture added to red wine and heated for the third time.

SERVES 6–10	6 cloves
1 litre (1¼ pints) aquavit or vodka	5mm (¼in) piece of cinnamon stick
1 bottle red wine	4 strips orange peel
6 cardamom pods	225g (8oz) lump sugar

Place the aquavit and wine with the spices and orange peel in a pan over a medium heat. Simmer very gently for 1 hour, covered, to infuse the flavours. Put the lump sugar on a wire rack and balance it over the pan. Fill a ladle with the glogg, light with a match, and pour over the sugar. Continue this process until the sugar has dissolved, then stir thoroughly. Serve hot.

A tip: put a small metal spoon into the glass before you pour in the hot liquid, and this will prevent the glass from cracking.

MEAD

*Meade is made of honney and water boyled together, if it be fyned
and pure it preserveth helth.*   Anon

Mead is fermented honey water, a by-product of beekeeping. It
evolved from metheglin, which in turn came from hydromel, a
favourite drink of the Greeks and Romans. According to Lord
Holles, an Elizabethan gentleman, a cup of this honey mixed with
spring water and ginger, taken at night, 'will cure thee of all troubles'.
Metheglin was also said to promote and preserve good health. As
early as the sixth century it was an important drink in Russia, and it
seems to crop up in many parts of the world: the Indian word for
mead is *Madhu*, the Lithuanian *Medus*, the German *Meth*.

Whereas metheglin used a strong-flavoured honey, the best
mead was made with a mild one. It was made from the washings
of honeycombs after the honey had been extracted, and rainwater gave the best results. Beebread – a mixture of pollen and
nectar predigested by the bees – was used as a fermentation
agent. Monks took pride in developing special cultures of yeast for
their mead, which they guarded jealously down the years.
Everyone's mead had a subtle difference to it, the flower fragrance
was selected to enhance the brew, and much pride was taken in
its culture.

18th-century Recipe for Mead

*To 1 gallon of water take 1 pint honey. Boil it, and after boiling,
immediately plunge in a handful of rosemary, sweet briar or a little
lemon balm. A bay leaf, or some cloves and bruised ginger, may be added
if liked, but we do not care for mead in which the taste of the honey is
burnt out with ginger and spices.*
Dorothy Hartley, *Food in England*

The brew was then fermented until it stopped 'working', and
skimmed. It was poured into a cask with some raisins, bunged and
left to rest for 3 months. It could be 'drawn off in frosty weather,
when it will be found very clear and bright, with a fine froth'.

A Finnish friend makes hers with the addition of lemon rind,
which sounds delicious.

An apiculturist in traditional protective costume.

POSSETS AND CAUDELS

A posset was drunk from a posset-cup, a specially made china dish with a cover. It is a drink of hot milk curdled with ale, wine or some other liquor and often flavoured with sugar and spices. It was prescribed for catarrh, colds and other minor ailments, as described in a couplet by Dryden:

A sparing diet did her health assure
Or sick, a posset was her cure.

Dr Johnson describes posset as 'milk curdled with wine and other acids' and they came in various forms: milk-possets, pepper-possets, cider-possets or egg-possets.

A Simple but Brilliant Posset

600ml (1 pint) milk
150ml (¼ pint) white wine
50g (2oz) cube sugar
1 lemon, unwaxed
1 teaspoon ground ginger
Grated nutmeg

Bring the milk to the boil in a pan, then add the wine. Set aside for 10 minutes to curdle. Strain off the curds. Rub the sugar over the lemon and stir into the hot curds. Flavour with the ground ginger and nutmeg to taste. It is unbelievably delicious.

A richer recipe suggests heating raw cane sugar with sherry and nutmeg, adding eggs until they cook, then milk. The mixture is heated through and served thick and hot.

Caudels

These are a kind of gruel, a mixture of eggs, cereals and malt serving as a food-drink combination to see folk through long journeys or extended gaps between meals. Sometimes they were made with beer, sometimes with whisky or other spirits. Caudels were warming and nourishing and kept you going until you landed a solid meal. They were made in countless ways, but here is one based on a description by Charles Dickens:

A Victorian posset-cup.

A Dickensian Caudel

2 tablespoons medium oatmeal
600ml (1 pint) hot water
Thinly pared rind of half a lemon
50g (2oz) sugar
¼ teaspoon ground nutmeg
½ teaspoon ginger
1 egg, beaten
1–2 tablespoons brandy

Stir the oatmeal into the water with the lemon rind and boil until thick. Strain through a nylon sieve, add the sugar and spices and mix in the beaten egg. Return to the pan and heat very gently for 2 minutes. Finish with the brandy.

Alternatively, according to a Scottish recipe, you can cook the oatmeal in milk, and use whisky rather than brandy. Or you can use cinnamon and a blade of mace to spice it, and use mild ale or porter, a dark brown malt beer instead of water.

A feminine version was made with ground rice, port and ginger.

SYLLABUBS

'Bub' is sixteenth-century slang for a bubbling drink, traditionally made by mixing wine and brandy with whipped frothing cream. Sill was a region of Champagne which provided the bubbles. An instant 'syllabub under the cow' was made by drawing the milk from the cow directly on to the wine. An Irishwoman told me of a family tradition dating back to the seventeenth century whereby her ancestors used to attend a well-dressing in May. Every member of the family would gather at the well early in the morning with a flask or vessel containing a measure of whisky, on to which the cow was milked.

In the seventeenth and eighteenth centuries the syllabub developed various forms: a punch bowl of cider or ale, spiced with cinnamon and nutmeg, was sweetened with sugar and the milkmaid milked the cow on to it to produce an alcoholic whey, which was sometimes served with cream on top. A syllabub made with wine or spirits was a richer mixture, containing four-fifths cream and spooned rather than drunk out of glasses. Then someone discovered that if you reduced the proportion of wine and sugar to cream, it would not separate: this became the basis of the 'Everlasting Syllabub'.

You can also make syllabubs with syrups rather than alcohol (see page 176). In the nineteenth century they were sometimes made with the juice of Seville oranges.

An Everlasting Syllabub

Most syllabubs are as delicious to drink as they are to eat from a spoon. I have thickened this one with double cream for a luxurious satin texture.

> *1 lemon*
> *125ml (4fl oz) sherry or white wine*
> *2 tablespoons brandy*
> *50g (2oz) caster sugar*
> *300ml (½ pint) double cream*
> *Whole nutmeg*
> *2 egg whites*
> *Small edible rose petals, to decorate*
> *Caster sugar*

Pare the lemon rind thinly and put into a bowl with the wine and brandy. Leave for several hours or overnight.

Strain into another bowl. Add the sugar and stir until dissolved. Pour in the cream slowly, beating all the time with a wire whisk. Grate in a little nutmeg and fold in one stiffly whisked egg white. Spoon into small glasses and keep in a cool place (not the fridge) until ready to eat. The syllabub can be made 2–3 days in advance. Decorate just before serving with rose-petals dipped in egg white then frosted with caster sugar.

Syllabub Trifle

A dessert of taboos, wickedly crammed with cream and alcohol. Completely irresistible.

> SERVES 6–8
> *1 home-made sponge cake, broken into pieces*
> *3 tablespoons sherry and 2 tablespoons brandy, mixed*
> *300ml (½ pint) single cream*
> *4 tablespoons caster sugar*
> *4 large free-range eggs*
> *5 tablespoons mango purée, sweetened to taste*
> *150ml (¼ pint) sherry*
> *3 tablespoons caster sugar*
> *4 tablespoons brandy*
> *Juice of half lemon*
> *300ml (½ pint) double cream*
> *25g (1oz) slivered almonds*

Line the base of a large glass bowl with the sponge pieces, and moisten with the sherry and brandy. Heat the single cream. Beat the sugar into the eggs until creamy, then pour on the hot cream. Return to the pan over a low heat, just long enough to thicken to a custard, taking care not to let it boil and curdle. Cool, then pour over the sponge layer. When cold, spoon the mango purée over the top.

Mix the sherry, sugar, nutmeg, brandy and lemon juice. Beat in the cream slowly with a wire whisk until it thickens. Chill for several hours or overnight.

Just before serving, pour the syllabub over the top of the trifle and sprinkle with slivered almonds.

An Everlasting Syllabub.

PUNCHES

The origin of the word punch is thought to come from the Persian *punj*, or the Sanskrit *panca*, meaning five, denoting the number of ingredients – spirits, sugar, lemon, spices and water or milk. Special punch bowls became quite an art-form in silverware and china, with ladles to match made of silver mounted on wooden handles so as not to conduct heat. Families had their own special recipes for punch which were handed down through the generations, and which were served on special family occasions.

Mrs Beeton comments in her original volume of *Household Management* that 'it is thought to be very intoxicating ... but its strength does not appear to the taste to be so great as it really is. Punch, which was universally drunk among the middle classes about 50 or 60 years ago, has almost disappeared from our domestic tables, being superseded by wine.'

This is her recipe (I decorate it with slices of orange):

½ pint rum   1 large lemon
½ pint brandy   ½ teaspoon nutmeg
¼ lb sugar   1 pint boiling water

Rub the sugar over the lemon until it has absorbed all the yellow part of the skin, then put the sugar into a punchbowl. Add the lemon juice (free from pips), and mix these two ingredients well together. Pour over them the boiling water, stir well together, add the rum, brandy and nutmeg; mix thoroughly, and the punch will be ready to serve. It is very important in making a good punch that all the ingredients are thoroughly incorporated; and to insure success, the processes of mixing must be diligently attended to.

German Punch

This recipe, a favourite of my German friend Inge, is traditionally served on Christmas Eve as the family gathers for the festive rituals.

SERVES 10   2 small sticks cinnamon
175g (6oz) sugar   6 cloves
300ml (½ pint) water   1 bottle Moselle or Hock
Pared rinds of half a lemon   1 bottle red wine
    and half an orange   3 wine glasses of brandy

Heat the sugar, water, rinds and spices in a large pan, stirring until the sugar dissolves. Cover and leave to infuse over a very low heat for 30–40 minutes. Add the wines and the brandy, heat through again, remove from the heat and serve.

Mrs Beeton wrote, in her original edition of Household Management, that punches are 'very intoxicating'.

A Norwegian non-alcoholic punch.

Jesus College Milk Punch

This is served on the annual occasion of the Audit Feast in Jesus College Cambridge, at the end of a considerable intake of food and fine wines. According to the Manciple (head steward) not all that much is drunk, and it sits on the side cooling, acquiring a nasty-looking crust on top. It is, however, a delicious drink.

SERVES 10	3 egg yolks
1 lemon	*1.8 litres (3 pints) milk*
20cl (½ pint) brandy	*225g (8oz) sugar*
100ml (4fl oz) noyau (Amaretto)	*35cl (¼ pint) rum*
Freshly grated nutmeg	

Peel the rind of the lemon thinly and place in a tumbler. Pour over it a little brandy and noyau with a little grated nutmeg, cover with a saucer and let it stand for about 8 hours. Beat the egg yolks with a little cold milk. Put the remaining milk in a pan and bring to the boil. Stir in the yolks, sugar, rum and remaining brandy and noyau and the lemon rind mixture. Continue to stir until it thickens. Strain off into a punch bowl and grate over it a little nutmeg.

Non-alcoholic Punch

If you prefer a non-alcoholic punch, this recipe from friends in Norway is a delicious drink.

675g (1½lb) icing sugar	*1 teaspoon grated nutmeg*
2 litres (3 ½ pints) water	*1 litre (1¼ pints) boiling milk*
Juice of 8 lemons	*Frozen grapes, to serve*
Grated rind of 4 lemons	

Place the sugar and water in a pan and bring to the boil. Boil, uncovered, for 5 minutes. Cool, then add the lemon juice, peel and nutmeg. Leave to stand overnight.

Stir the boiling milk into the lemon mixture, and leave to stand for 24 hours. Strain through cheesecloth and pour the cold punch into bottles.

Serve cold, adding this mouthwatering touch: freeze some grapes in advance and float them in the drink.

Whisky Punch

From a friend in Scotland who was interested in this section of the book and wanted to share an ancestral recipe. 'The most fascinating tipple ever invented', goes his message. Just mix the ingredients together.

600ml (1 pint) whisky	*1 wine glass of boiling ale*
2 glasses brandy	*225g (8oz) sugar*
Juice and rind of 1 lemon	*1.2 litres (2 pints) boiling water*

SYRUPS AND CORDIALS

You can make a range of old-fashioned syrups from fruits and herbs to use in contemporary ways, such as sodas, wine cups and certain dessert sauces. They are simple to do, and can be stored indefinitely in a cool place. They should be bottled in warm bottles while hot, and corked immediately. Keep cold or refridgerated for up to six months.

Almond Syrup

Miles of almond groves line the road in parts of California. A friend made us a soda with her home-made almond syrup when we visited, and it was sublime.

225g (8oz) sweet almonds,	*600ml (1 pint) cold water*
blanched and skinned	*350g (12oz) cube sugar*
30ml (1fl oz) almond essence	

Grind the almonds roughly in a food processor. Place in a pan with the almond essence and stir in the water. Add the sugar and bring to the boil. Simmer for 3 minutes, then strain through a linen bag. It may need straining twice.

Coffee Syrup

An Italian friend sent me this amazing recipe from Venice. Try pouring it over praline ice-cream, or mixing it with crème fraîche to go with a chocolate gâteau.

450g (1lb) freshly ground coffee	*450g (1lb) sugar*
600ml (1 pint) water	

Bring the coffee and water to the boil in a pan and boil for 20 minutes. Strain through muslin and stir in the sugar. When it has dissolved, return to the pan and simmer, skim and simmer again until the syrup becomes thick.

Cassis

Blackcurrant syrup is widely used in France: a dash in white wine for kir, or a splash over ice-cream to transform it. A good friend who lives in Cucuron in South-East France sent me her version, to which she sometimes adds brandy before bottling. In autumn, she makes it with blackberries, or bilberries if she can find them.

Coffee syrup is delicious poured over ice-cream.

2.25kg (5lb) blackcurrants	*300ml (½ pint) cold water*
900g (2lb) cube sugar	

Put the berries and sugar into a stoneware jar or crock, bruise the fruit and leave overnight, covered with a cloth.

Stir the fruit, add the water and stand the jar in a pot of boiling water. Boil gently for 2½ hours. Strain through muslin, then boil for 5–10 minutes.

Lemon or Orange Syrup

One of the most refreshing of all syrups, this is wonderful in summer weather. My uncle, who lived for a while in southern Spain, sent me this recipe.

1.8kg (3lb) cube sugar
2.5 litres (4 pints) boiling water
Juice of 5 lemons or oranges
Finely pared rind of 3 lemons
or oranges
100g (4oz) citric acid

Put the sugar and water into a preserving pan. Add the juice and rind. Dissolve the citric acid in a little hot water and pour into the mixture. Leave to stand for 24 hours, then strain and bottle.

Rose Red Syrup

A delightful and delicious combination from the grandmother of a Frenchwoman who now lives in Normandy. It is a rich red colour and has a heavenly flavour.

450g (1lb) redcurrants
1.2 litres (2 pints) cold water
900g (2lb) cube sugar
450g (1lb) scented red rose petals,
trimmed of the white 'heel'

Simmer the currants in the water for 20–25 minutes until all the juice is extracted, then strain. Add the sugar and the rose petals. Simmer gently for 15 minutes, then strain off the rose petals. Boil until the syrup thickens.

Elderflower Cordial

For many years now I have been making elderflower cordial for my family. Every June, when the elder produces its plentiful crop of flowers, I am out there to gather them – although European folklore warns against the elder mother who will wreak her revenge if you harm the tree. So it is as well to appease her before you pick.

20 heads of elderflower
1.5 kg (3 ½lb) sugar
1.8 litres (3 pints) boiled water, cold
50g (2oz) tartaric acid
1 lemon, sliced

Put all the ingredients into a large pan and leave to steep, stirring occasionally, for 24 hours. Strain and bottle. It is ready to drink immediately, but keeps for several weeks. Dilute with mineral water.

Bramble Cordial

The bramble gets its name from 'brom' or thorny shrub, and in Germany it is still called *brombeere*. As well as its culinary uses, the root of the bramble provides an orange dye.

To every 600ml (1 pint) blackberry juice (below) you need:

1.8–2.25kg (4–5lb) blackberries
225g (8oz) sugar
1 stick cinnamon
3–4 cloves
Rind of half a lemon

For the blackberry juice: wash the blackberries and put them into a preserving pan with no added water. Heat slowly until the juice runs freely, but don't let them boil. Strain through a jelly bag and leave to drip.

Measure the juice into a large pan. Add the sugar, spices and lemon rind and boil for 30 minutes. Strain off and bottle. You can add whisky or vodka if you want an alcoholic version.

Summer Cordial of Soft Fruits

A stunning way of using summer fruits in high season. You can add a quantity of brandy, to taste, to make an alcoholic drink.

Blackcurrants, redcurrants, raspberries, strawberries and so on
Water   *Brandy*   *Sugar*

Put the fruit into a stoneware jar and stand it in boiling water until the juice has run from the fruit. Strain off and measure. Add 450g (1lb) sugar for every 600ml (1 pint) of juice. Mix well. Allow to stand, covered, for several days, then strain again and bottle.

Rose-red syrup.

DRINKS TO CHEER THE POORLY

When I was writing a book about village life I came across a woman who had worked 'below stairs' as a maid in the manor house nearby during the 1920s and 30s. Although she is now frail and her memory poor, she handed me a couple of handwritten notebooks with all the tips and recipes she had collected from those long-gone days. 'Invalids require variety', she had been told. 'The drinks succeed each other in different forms and flavours.' Evidently looking after invalids was an art-form in those days. I tried them out and they are excellent. Give your patient a selection of these stunning recipes, lightly edited for today.

Three Agreeable Drinks

• Into a tumbler of cold water, pour 1 tablespoon of lemon juice.
• Scald currants or cranberries, strain, and add a little sugar to taste.
• Serve buttermilk with biscuits or rusks, and ripe or dried fruits, raisins in particular.

Apple Water

Slice and bake 2 large apples and pour on 1.2 litres (2 pints) of boiling water. Leave to stand for 2–3 hours then strain. Sweeten lightly with honey.

Barley Water

Wholesome and nourishing, lovely when you feel too ill to eat much.

Wash a handful of barley, then simmer it gently in 1.8 litres (3 pints) of water with a bit of lemon rind.

Or boil 25g (1oz) pearl barley in a little water for a few minutes, to cleanse, then strain. Put the barley in a pan with 1.2 litres (2 pints) of water and simmer for 1 hour. When half done add a piece of fresh lemon rind and a cube of sugar. If it seems to be too thick, you may add another 150ml (¼ pint of water). Lemon juice may be added if chosen.

Chocolate

This is the best hot chocolate I've ever tasted. Sure to uplift the spirits and strengthen a weak body.

Break 200g (7oz) of plain chocolate into very small pieces. Heat 300ml (½ pint) of water in the pot and when it boils put in the chocolate. Stir it off the fire until quite melted, then heat on a gentle fire till it boils. Pour it into a bowl. It will keep in a cool place for 8–10 days, or more. When wanted, put a spoonful or two into a cup of milk, boil it with sugar, and stir it well.

Artificial Asses Milk

This is wonderfully soothing and settling.

Mix together 2 tablespoons of boiling water, 2 tablespoons of milk, and an egg, well beaten. Sweeten with 2 tablespoons of white sugar. Take twice or thrice a day.

Coffee Milk

A beautiful way of reviving the poorly – a sweet 'caffe latte'.

Boil a dessertspoon of ground coffee in 300ml (½ pint) of milk for 15 minutes. Let it boil for a few minutes and set it on the side of the fire to grow fine. Strain, then sweeten to taste.

the saucepan, put it on a gentle fire, stir it one way for not more than a minute, for if it boil, or the egg be stale, it will curdle. Serve with toast.

Ground Rice Milk

Comforting for the stomach, pleasant and easy to drink with delicious spicing.

Boil 1 heaped tablespoon of ground rice with 300ml (½ pint) milk, ¼ teaspoon each of cinnamon, lemon rind and nutmeg. Sweeten to taste when nearly done.

Lemon Water

A delightful pick-me-up. It's like lemon tea and makes a nice change from ordinary tea.

Put 2 slices of lemon into a teapot with a little bit of rind, and a cube of sugar. Pour in 600ml (1 pint) of boiling water and leave, covered, for 2 hours before drinking.

Lemon Wheys

This cleansing drink is an excellent remedy for a queasy stomach.

Pour into 300ml (½ pint) boiling milk the juice of half a lemon. Leave to stand for 15 minutes until a small quantity is quite clear. Strain off through muslin and put in a cube of sugar.

Soft and Fine Draught for Those Who are Weak and Have a Cough

A lovely potion, light and flowery yet nourishing and comforting. Far nicer than most cough mixtures.

Beat an egg and mix it well with 150ml (¼ pint) of warm milk, 1 tablespoon each of rose-water and orange-flower water, and a little grated nutmeg. Do not warm it after the egg is put in. Take it first thing in the morning and last thing at night.

Egg Wine

Not unlike zabaglione, this is soothing, comforting food.

Beat an egg, and mix with a teaspoon of cold water. Set on the fire a glass (75ml/2½fl oz) of white wine, half a glass of water, 1 tablespoon sugar and ½ teaspoon nutmeg. When this boils, pour a little of it on to the egg by degrees till the whole be in, stirring it well. Then return the whole into

Pleasant to Drink

Sharp and uplifting, and full of vitamin C.

Put a teacupful of cranberries into a cup of water and mash them. In the meantime, boil 1.2 litres (2 pints) of water with 1 tablespoon of oatmeal and a bit of lemon rind, then add the cranberries and sugar to taste. Add about 150ml (¼ pint) of sherry, or less, as may be proper. Boil the whole for 30 minutes and strain.

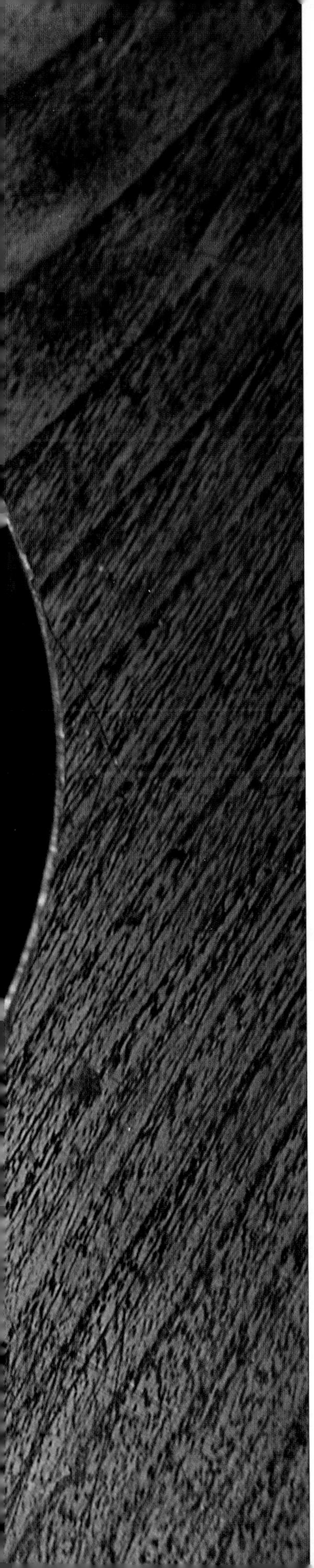

NIGHTCAPS

Fine orange well roasted, with wine in a cup,
They'll make a sweet bishop when gentlefolks sup.
Swift

One of the oldest recipes for a nightcap is bishop, famous in – among other places – the University of Oxford. It was and is a drink of sweetened wine or port with oranges and lemons and sugar. The following recipe comes from *Oxford Nightcaps*, of 1827. My father, who was a proctor in the university for a short term in the 1930s, recalled a similar drink being served after a Feast at High Table.

Using sherry instead of port, this drink was curiously called lawn sleeves. For cardinal use claret, whereas for pope use champagne. Norwegian friends make what they call old-fashioned bishop (*Gammeldags bisp*), using sweetened red wine with oranges.

Bishop

1 orange	*1 blade mace*	*400ml (14fl oz) port*
15 cloves	*6 allspice berries*	*6–10 sugar lumps*
Short stick cinnamon	*Piece of root ginger, bruised*	*1 lemon*
12 cloves	*300 ml (½ pint) water*	*Nutmeg*

Prick the orange in several places and stick with the cloves. Roast in the oven at 200°C/400°F/gas 6 for 30 minutes. Put the spices in a pan with the water and boil until reduced by half.

Heat the port to drive off some of the alcohol, then add the roasted orange and the hot spice mixture. Leave to stand over a very low heat for 10 minutes.

Rub the sugar lumps over the lemon and add to the mixture. Stir, grate a little fresh nutmeg over the top and serve.

Rumfustian

This was a thick drink enriched with egg yolks: the mixture of alcohol would knock anyone unconscious and I'm not sure that I would recommend it. For purely academic interest, the recipe goes:

12 egg yolks, 1.2 litres (2 pints) strong beer, 1 bottle of wine, 600ml (1 pint) of gin, and cinnamon, nutmeg, sugar and ginger to taste. Beat and warm (without boiling which would curdle the egg yolks) until thick.

Oxford Nightcaps also recommends:

Brown Betty

Brown sugar, dissolved in 1 pint of hot water, a slice of lemon in it. Add cloves, cinnamon, brandy and a quart of strong ale. Heat it up, and float a round of brown toast on top of it – and on the toast grate nutmeg and ginger root. Serve hot.

Bishop.

BEER

Pliny advises that five almonds consumed before drinking ale will preserve sobriety. Hops were not used in beer-making until the sixteenth century. Before this the traditional country drink in many parts of the world was ale, which was brewed from malt and yeast and flavoured with herbs. Forty per cent of the Sumerian grain crop went into beer production, so popular was ale, and the brewers were women. In Russia, 'kvas' has been an important national drink since the sixth century AD, made from malted barley or rye.

Malt is made by steeping barley grains in water so that they begin to germinate, then heating them to arrest the process: the longer they are heated, the darker the malt. Soft water was generally considered to give the best results in beer-making, and the flavourings used before the arrival of hops included hay, bog myrtle (sweet gale), mugwort, wormwood, rosemary and ground ivy which had a common country name of ale-hoof.

Eventually ale and beer became synonymous. The strongest beer was brewed for special and festive occasions, whereas the light beer brewed for harvest workers was as inoffensive as barley water. Every household would make its own beer to serve its own purpose, and the brewing copper was used as regularly as the bread oven.

Nettle Beer

A light, tasty beer for hot summer days, this beer has been a tradition in country households for centuries.

A large basket full of fresh	450g (1lb) sugar
young nettle tops	25g (1oz) ginger
1 lemon, cut up	25g (1oz) cream of tartar
4.5 litres (8 pints) water	25g (1oz) brewer's yeast

Put the nettle tops and lemon in a large pan with the water and boil for 25 minutes. Strain into a wooden tub, add the sugar, ginger and cream of tartar and stir until dissolved. Add the yeast and leave in a warm place to ferment for 3 days, or longer if the weather is chilly. Store in a small cask or bottle for immediate use.

Bell-ringers' Beer Flip

To drink before a long peal – presumably to warm, sustain and inspire. Adapted from Dorothy Hartley, *Food in England*.

8 eggs, separated
Sugar, orange juice and spices
1.2 litres (2 pints) strong beer, heated

Beat the egg yolks with sugar, orange juice and spices and pour on the hot beer. Then pour it back into the pan from a great height so that it froths. Add the stiffly beaten egg whites to the froth, and serve immediately.

Tankards

The serious beer *aficionado*, keeps his beer tankard – pewter of course – in the same place as the beer, because pewter at room temperature will make the beer seem unpleasantly warm. Traditionally, pewter tankards, with a jug of beer, were served on a wooden tray for the effect of the musical sound of pewter on wood. The tankards were kept well-polished, the trays well-scoured.

Pewter tankards should be washed in warm soapy water, dried, then polished with a soft cloth. In the old days they were cleaned with fine sifted sand and coarse rushes. Today a scouring pad will do the job, but do not use metal polishes or chemicals on pewter since it retains odours and will contaminate the beer.

Bell-ringers' beer flip.

CIDER

Cider on beer makes good cheer
Beer on cider makes a bad rider

Cider often replaces beer in apple-growing areas. English country lore has it that late frosts on 19–21 May, which often destroy the year's crop of apples, occur because a brewer called Franklin from Devon sold his soul to the Devil for frost on those three days, so that people would buy his beer instead of drinking cider.

Cider-making was the domain of the farmer's wife, and a cider press was as often as not shared around a district, and trundled around from farm to farm during the autumn. The farmer would sometimes give cider to his workers in part payment. Cider-making is a far simpler process than brewing beer: all you need is apples, something to pulp them with, and a wooden barrel. Traditionally, apple-pressing began on November 1st, although it now begins in September. Most of the work is done by Christmas, although it can continue until March if there are enough apples.

There are numerous varieties of cider apples, but Bramleys and Laxtons are considered by many to make the best cider. They need no addition – although some ghastly 'improvers' have been used in the past, from blood, milk or cream to a rain-soaked rag and a dead sheep. No sugar is added to rough cider, but vintage cider is made with sugar and is left to mature for longer.

Rough Cider

Pulp the apples, press out the juice, and put it into wooden barrels. Leave to stand in the orchard for 6 months.

Cider Cup

In a pan heat 600ml (1 pint) dry cider, 2 wine glasses brandy, 3 tablespoons sugar and the juice of half a lemon, and stir over a low heat for 5 minutes. Grate some nutmeg on to 2 slices of lemon and float on top of the cup. Serve chilled.

Farmhouse Wines

Ever since the principle of fermentation was discovered, way back in antiquity, wines have been made by country people the world over. Home-made wines were always, and still are today, made from almost anything plentiful in the garden: soft fruits, rhubarb, plums, apples, pears and quinces. From the vegetable patch, beetroot, carrot, marrow, celery and pea-pods all make excellent traditional wines.

In the early days, rural wine-making equipment was simple: an earthenware 'panshon' to start the wine, a pestle and mortar to bruise and break the spices, old spirit casks for fermentation, and whatever bottles were around – always sterilized. Today, winemakers prefer large glass jars or plastic bins, fitted with fermentation traps. Be sure to sterilize all equipment and keep the first ferment well covered against fruit flies – they turn the wine to vinegar! Use a yeast nutrient to make sure of a good fermentation. Country wines make full use of natural yeasts found on plants and fruits, so many of the recipes do not add extra yeast: when they do, they traditionally spread it on toast and float it on top of the working wine. Even this was not wasted, as an eighteenth-century manuscript tells us: 'The toasts taken out of ale and wine should always be given to the hens – it will encourage them mightily.'

Parsnip wine (see page 186).

Bread Wine

Records show that the ancient Egyptians made wine from bread, and this very early manuscript recipe gives a version made with rye bread and honey, to make a sweet wine resembling mead. This version was passed down through a family living near Tours in France.

900g (2lb) loaf of home-made bread, broken up

450g (1lb) sugar
3.5 litres (6 pints) water

Brown the bread lightly in a low oven at 150°C/300°F/gas 2 for 30–40 minutes. Cool, then put into a wine jar. Dissolve the sugar in the water and pour over the bread. Keep the jar in a warm place until well fermented. Drain off into a cask. Bung lightly until the fermentation is complete, then bottle.

Keep for 3–4 months before drinking – it will improve with time. It is a lively, heady wine.

Dandelion Wine

This recipe comes from the man to whom I owe the idea for this book: he is now in his nineties, so this wine has seen many successful seasons. Thank you, Harry!

1 orange
1 lemon
3.75 litres (6 pints) dandelion flowers

4.8 litres (1 gallon) water
1.4kg (3lb) sugar
25g (1oz) brewer's yeast

Peel the orange and lemon, with as little pith as possible. Put the peel and dandelion heads into a muslin bag and boil in the water for 20 minutes. Remove the bag, squeeze lightly and dissolve the sugar in the liquid. Pour into a plastic bucket (not metal) and when lukewarm (not cold) add the juice of the orange and lemon. Mix the yeast with a little of the liquid and pour back into the bucket and cover.

Irish 'poteen' or potato wine.

Leave to work for 3 days, then syphon into a fermentation jar, and leave until it has finished fermenting. When fermentation has quite finished, bottle it up. The longer the wine is kept the better it will taste.

Parsnip Wine

One of the oldest and most traditional of country wines. This recipe is from a Dutch friend living on a farm in the south Netherlands.

1.8kg (4lb) parsnips, cut up *1.5kg (3lb) demerara sugar*
4.8 litres (8 pints) boiling water *1 tablespoon fresh yeast*
25g (1oz) root ginger, cinnamon, *A slice of toasted bread*
allspice and mace, to taste

Boil the parsnips in the water for 15 minutes. Add the bruised or broken spices and stir gently for a further 10 minutes. Strain, add the sugar and stir to dissolve. Leave it until lukewarm. Spread the yeast on to the toast and float on the liquid. Allow it to work for about 36 hours (longer if the weather is cool), then pour it into a cask and leave to ferment. As soon as fermentation ceases, bung securely and leave for 6 months. Rack off into bottles and store for a year before using. It improves with time – a 10-year-old parsnip wine is very fine.

Potato Wine

This recipe was sent to me by an Irishman who described the 'poteen' (potato spirit) that his grandfather brewed (illegally!). This wine is the legal version.

900g (2lb) potatoes, scrubbed *600ml (1 pint) fresh wheat,*
clean *husked*
900g (2lb) raisins *19 litres (4 gallons) boiling water*
1.8kg (4lb) demerara sugar *25g (1oz) yeast*

Grate the potatoes into a large pan, add the rest of the ingredients and stir at regular intervals for 3 weeks. Strain off into a keg to ferment, then rack and bottle.

HEDGEROW WINES

Our ancestors always made wine from what grew around them in the wild: nettles, gorse, coltsfoot and clover made fragrant flower wines. Cowslip was the most famous of all, but these flowers, so over-picked, are no longer abundant enough to use. Hawthorn, rowan, bilberry, damson, sloe and crab-apple make heady fruit wines. Picked at the peak of their ripeness, they were used as soon as possible after picking. Autumn berries are considered best after the second hard frost, spring water is used whenever possible, and it is important never to use aluminium or iron pans because it spoils the colour of the wine. A wooden cask was traditionally thought best for fermentation, or earthenware, although nowadays it is usually glass. The weather dictated the time to rack the wine 'when the frost has stilled and cleared the standing water in the pond, it will have stilled and cleared the wine in the cellar', says country wisdom. For utmost clarity, decant hedgerow wines before drinking.

Elderberry Wine

Every wine-maker appears to have his or her version of how to make this excellent hedgerow wine. This particular version comes from a German doctor who inherited the recipe from his grandfather. There are many superstitions about the elder tree, including the one that a powerful Dryad, the Elder-mother, inhabits it and you should respectfully ask her permission to gather its fruit or flowers.

2kg (4lb) elderberries	3 teaspoons citric acid
4.5 litres (1 gallon) water	1 sachet wine yeast (Port type)
225g (8oz) raisins	1.5kg (3½ lb) sugar

Strip the berries from their stalks, wash them clean in cold water and remove every trace of stalk and unripe berry. Place the berries in a suitable sterilized vessel, crush them and pour boiling

Elderberries.

water over them. Wash and chop the raisins and add to the vessel together with the acid. Cover and leave until cool.

Add the wine yeast and ferment on the pulp for three days, then strain out. Press and discard the fruit, stir in the sugar, pour the must into a sterilized fermentation jar and the excess into a large bottle, likewise sterilized. Fit an airlock into the jar and a plug of cotton wool to the bottle and leave them in a warm room until the wine is still – about three weeks. Move the wine to a cold place for a few days to help it to clear, then siphon it into a sterilized storage jar and another bottle. Bung tightly and keep for one year before bottling, then keep for a further six months before drinking. This is a strong, slightly sweet wine to serve after meals.

Blackberry Wine

One of the most frequently made of hedgerow wines because of the abundance of the blackberry harvest, this version was given to me by a local farmer's wife whose grandmother made it before her. It is invaluable, she swears, as a tonic, and as a medicine for winter ailments.

Crush the berries, and pour on 1.2 litres (2 pints) boiling water to each 4.8 litres (8 pints) fruit. Let the mixture stand for 24 hours, stirring occasionally. Strain and measure into a keg, adding 900g (2lb) sugar, and 600ml (1 pint) rye whisky to each gallon. Cork tightly, and let it stand for about 2 months before drinking.

Blackberries

Wild Rose-hips

Wild Rose-hip Wine

Here is one answer to using up the abundant annual harvest of rose-hips. A fine hedgerow wine, dry and distinctive. From a villager in East Anglia.

Hips	Water	Sugar

Pick the rose-hips when quite ripe. Take off the stalks, mash them, cover and leave for a day. Drain well in a fine sieve, squeezing out all the juice. Measure, and to every 1.2 litres (2 pints) juice add 225g (8oz) sugar. Cover, and leave for a day, stirring now and then to make sure the sugar has dissolved. Put into a cask that just holds the amount of wine. Bung the hole lightly. When it no longer hisses close the bunghole tightly and leave for 3 months. Then bottle, and leave to mature for 6–9 months at least. It will improve the longer it is kept.

LIST OF RECIPES

INDEX

Photographic acknowledgements

All photographs by Michelle Garrett except for:
A–Z Botannical Collection Limited: 8–9, Björn Svensson; 10, Mark Bolton; 14, Houses and Interiors; 110–11 (bee skep) Kellie Castle.
Christie's Images: 166 *Loving Cup* by Daniel Maclise R.A.
Melanie Eclare: 57, 78–9 (background).
Ecoscene: 25 top, Ian Beames; 46 top, David Wootton.
FLPA: 88, Cath Mullen.
Foulsham Press for facsimile of *Old Moore's Almanack* on page 47.
The Garden Picture Library: 40, Juliette Wade; 50–1 John Miller; 54, JS Sira; 55, John Glover; 98, Clive Boursnell; 114 and 116, John Glover; 118 (above), Jerry Pavia;
    119 and 148 (right), Ron Sutherland; 149 (left), Tim Spence, (right), Nigel Francis; 156 (above), Vaughan Fleming; 184, Tim Macmillan; 187, Sunniva Harte; 188 (top)
    Linda Burgess, (bottom), Howard Rice.
Michelle Garrett Archive: 6 (bottom), 7 (bottom), 13, 26, 30, 37, 41 (above), 42–3 (top and bottom), 45, 56 (bottom right), 58–9, (all three pictures), 61, 128, 148 (left)
    and 157.
Holt Studio International: 44, Willem Harinck; 115 (bottom left and right), 56 and 146 (bee), 164 and 170 (bee-keeper), Nigel Cattlin; 117, Primrose Peacock;
    118, (below) Bob Gibbons; 154, Phil McLean.
Jacqui Hurst: 28.